Stories of the Wagner Opera

by

H. A. Guerber

The Echo Library 2006

Published by

The Echo Library

Echo Library
131 High St.
Teddington
Middlesex TW11 8HH

www.echo-library.com

Please report serious faults in the text to complaints@echo-library.com

ISBN 1-40681-012-6

PREFACE.

These short sketches, which can be read in a few moments' time, are intended to give the reader as clear as possible an outline of the great dramatist-composer's work.

The author is deeply indebted to Professor G.T. Dippold, to Messrs. Forman, Jackman, and Corder, and to the Oliver Ditson Company, for the poetical quotations scattered throughout the text.

CONTENTS.

Page

Rienzi, the Last of the Tribunes

The Flying Dutchman

Tannhäuser

Lohengrin

Tristan and Ysolde

The Master-Singers of Nuremberg

The Nibelung's Ring.—Rheingold

The Walkyrie

Siegfried

Dusk of the Gods

Parsifal

RIENZI,

THE LAST OF THE TRIBUNES.

Wagner was greatly troubled in the beginning of his career about the choice of subjects for his operas. His first famous work, 'Rienzi,' is founded upon the same historical basis as Bulwer's novel bearing the same name, and is a tragic opera in five acts. The composer wrote the poem and the first two acts of the score in 1838, during his residence at Riga, and from there carried it with him to Boulogne. There he had an interview with Meyerbeer, after his memorable sea journey. Wagner submitted his libretto and the score for the first acts to that famous composer, who is reported to have said, 'Rienzi is the best opera-book extant,' and who gave him introductions to musical directors and publishers in Paris. In spite of this encouraging verdict on Meyerbeer's part, Wagner soon discovered that there was no chance of success for 'Rienzi' in France, and, after completing the score while dwelling at Meudon, he forwarded it in 1841 to Dresden. Here the opera found friends in the tenor Tichatscheck and the chorus-master Fisher, and when it was produced in 1842 it was received with great enthusiasm. The opera, which gave ample opportunity for great scenic display, was so long, however, that the first representation lasted from six o'clock to midnight. But when Wagner would fain have made excisions, the artists themselves strenuously opposed him, and preferred to give the opera in two successive evenings. At the third representation Wagner himself conducted with such success that 'he was the hero of the day.' This great triumph was reviewed with envy by the admirers of the Italian school of music, and some critics went so far in their partisanship as to denounce the score as 'blatant, and at times almost vulgar.' Notwithstanding these adverse criticisms, the opera continued to be played with much success at Dresden, and was produced at Berlin some years later, and at Vienna in 1871.

As Wagner's subsequent efforts have greatly surpassed this first work, 'Rienzi' is not often played, and has seldom been produced in America, I believe owing principally to its great length. The scene of 'Rienzi' is laid entirely in the streets and Capitol of Rome, in the middle of the fourteenth century, when the city was rendered unsafe by the constant dissensions and brawls among the noble families. Foremost among these conflicting elements were the rival houses of Colonna and Orsini, and, as in those days each nobleman kept an armed retinue within a fortified enclosure in town, he soon became a despot. Fearing no one, consulting only his own pleasure and convenience, he daily sallied forth to plunder, kidnap, and murder at his will. Such being the state of affairs, the streets daily flowed with blood; the merchants no longer dared open their shops and expose their wares lest they should be summarily carried away, and young and pretty women scarcely dared venture out of their houses even at noonday, lest they should be seen and carried away by noblemen.

Terrified by the lawlessness of the barons, whom he could no longer control, the Pope left Rome and took refuge at Avignon, leaving the ancient city a helpless prey to the various political factions which were engaged in continual strife. This state of affairs was so heart-rending that Rienzi, an unusually clever man of the people and an enthusiast, resolved to try and rouse the old patriotic spirit in the breast of the degenerate Romans, and to induce them to rise up against their oppressors and shake off their hated yoke.

Naturally a scholar and a dreamer, Rienzi would probably never have seen the necessity of such a thing, or ventured to attempt it, had he not seen his own little brother wantonly slain during one of the usual frays between the Orsini and Colonna factions. The murderer, a scion of the Colonna family, considered the matter as so trivial that he never even condescended to excuse himself, or to offer any redress to the injured parties, thus filling Rienzi's heart with a bitter hatred against all the patrician race. Secretly and in silence the young enthusiast matured his revolutionary plans, winning many adherents by his irresistible eloquence, and patiently bided his time until a suitable opportunity occurred to rally his partisans, openly defy the all-powerful barons, and restore the old freedom and prosperity to Rome.

The opera opens at nightfall, with one of the scenes so common in those days, an attempt on the part of the Orsini to carry off by force a beautiful girl from the presumably safe shelter of her own home. The street is silent and deserted, the armed band steal noiselessly along, place their scaling ladder under the fair one's casement, and the head of the Orsini, climbing up, seizes her and tries to carry her off in spite of her frantic cries and entreaties.

The noise attracts the attention of Adrian, heir of the Colonna family, and when he perceives that the would-be kidnappers wear the arms and livery of the Orsini, his hereditary foes, he seizes with joyful alacrity the opportunity to fight, and pounces upon them with all his escort. A confused street skirmish ensues, in the course of which Adrian rescues the beautiful maiden, whom he recognises as Irene, Rienzi's only sister. Attracted by the brawl, the people crowd around the combatants, cheering and deriding them with discordant cries, and becoming so excited that they refuse to disperse when the Pope's Legate appears and timidly implores them to keep the peace.

The tumult has reached a climax when Rienzi suddenly comes upon the scene, and authoritatively reminds his adherents that they have sworn to respect the law and the Church, and bids them withdraw. His words, received with enthusiastic cries of approbation by the people, are, however, scorned by the barons, who would fain continue the strife, but are forced to desist. Anxious to renew hostilities as soon as possible, and to decide the question of supremacy by the force of arms, the irate noblemen then and there appoint a time and place for a general encounter outside the city gates on the morrow, when they reluctantly disperse.

The appointment has been overheard by Rienzi, who, urged by the Legate of the Pope and by the clamours of the people to strike a decisive blow, decides to close the gates upon the nobles on the morrow, and to allow none to re-enter the city until they have taken a solemn oath to keep the peace and respect the law. In an impassioned discourse Rienzi then urges the people to uphold him now that the decisive moment has come, and to rally promptly around him at the sound of his trumpet, which will peal forth on the morrow to proclaim the freedom of Rome.

When they have all gone in obedience to his command, the Tribune, for such is the dignity which the people have conferred upon their champion Rienzi, turns toward the girl, the innocent cause of all the uproar, and perceives for the first time that it is his own sister Irene. Adrian is bending anxiously over her fainting form; but as soon as she recovers her senses she hastens to inform her brother that he saved her from Orsini's shameful attempt, and bespeaks his fervent thanks for her young protector.

It is then only that the Tribune realises that a Colonna, one of his bitterest foes, and one of the most influential among the hated barons, has overheard his instructions to his adherents, and can defeat his most secret and long cherished plans. Suddenly, however, he remembers that in youth he and Adrian often played together, and, counting upon the young nobleman's deep sense of honour, which he had frequently tested in the past, he passionately adjures him to show himself a true Roman and help him to save his unhappy country. Irene fervently joins in this appeal, and such is the influence of her beauty and distress that Adrian, who is very patriotic and who has long wished to see the city resume its former splendour, gladly consents to lend his aid.

This oath of allegiance received, Rienzi, whom matters of state call elsewhere, asks Adrian to remain in his house during his absence, to protect his sister against a renewal of the evening's outrage. Adrian joyfully accepts this charge, and the lovers, for they have been such from the very first glance exchanged, remain alone together and unite in a touching duet of faith and love, whose beautiful, peaceful strains contrast oddly with the preceding discordant strife. In spite of his transport at finding his affections returned, and in the very midst of his rapturous joy at embracing his beloved, Adrian, tortured by premonitory fears, warns Irene that her brother is far too sanguine of success, and that his hopes will surely be deceived. He also declares that he fears lest the proverbially fickle people may waver in their promised allegiance, and lest Rienzi may be the victim of the cruel barons whom he has now openly defied. The lovers' conversation is interrupted at sunrise by the ringing of the Capitol bell, proclaiming that the revolution has begun, and the triumphant chorus of priests and people is heard without, bidding all the Romans rejoice as their freedom is now assured. Riding ahead of the procession, Rienzi slowly passes by in the glittering armour and array of a Tribune, and from time to time pauses to address the crowd, telling them that the ancient city is once more free, and that he, as chief magistrate, will severely punish any and every infringement of the law. At the news of this welcome proclamation the enthusiasm of the people reaches such an exalted pitch that they all loudly swear to obey their Tribune implicitly, and loyally help him to uphold the might and dignity of the Holy City:—

'We swear to thee that great and free
Our Rome shall be as once of yore;

To protect it from tyranny
We'll shed the last drop of our gore.
Shame and destruction now we vow
To all the enemies of Rome;
A new free people are we now,
And we'll defend our hearth and home.'

The scene of the second act is laid in the Capitol, where the barons, who had been forced to take the oath of allegiance ere they were allowed to re-enter the city, are present, as well as the numerous emissaries from foreign courts. Heralds and messengers from all parts of the land crowd eagerly around the Tribune, anxious to do him homage, and to assure him that, thanks to his decrees, order and peace are now restored.

Amid the general silence the heralds make their reports, declaring that the roads are safe, all brigandage suppressed, commerce and agriculture more flourishing than ever before, a statement which Rienzi and the people receive with every demonstration of great joy. To the barons, however, these are very unwelcome tidings, and, knowing that the people could soon be cowed were they only deprived of their powerful leader, they gather together in one corner of the hall and plot how to put Rienzi to death.

Adrian accidentally discovers this conspiracy, and indignantly remonstrates with the barons, threatening even to denounce them, since they are about to break their word and resort to such dishonourable means. But his own father, Colonna, is one of the instigators of the conspiracy, and he dares him to carry out his threat, which would only result in branding him as a parricide. Then, without waiting to hear his son's decision, the old baron, accompanied by the other conspirators, joins Rienzi on the balcony, whence he has just addressed the assembled people. They have been listening to his last proposal, that the Romans should shake off the galling yoke of the German Empire and make their city a republic once more, and now loud and enthusiastic acclamations rend the air.

The speech ended, Adrian, stealing softly behind the Tribune, bids him be on the watch as treachery is lurking near. He has scarcely ended his warning and slipped away ere the conspirators suddenly surround the Tribune, and there, in the presence of the assembled people, they simultaneously draw their daggers, and strike him repeatedly. This dastardly attempt at murder utterly fails, however, as the Tribune wears a corselet of mail beneath the robes of state, and his guards quickly disarm and secure the conspirators while the people loudly clamour for their execution by the axe, a burly blacksmith, Cecco, acting as their principal spokesman.

Rienzi, who is principally incensed by their attack upon Roman liberties, and by their utter lack of faith, is about to yield to their demand, when Irene and Adrian suddenly fall at his feet, imploring the pardon of the condemned, and entreating him to show mercy rather than justice. Once more Rienzi addresses the people, but it requires all his persuasive eloquence to induce them, at last, to forgive the barons' attempt. Then the culprits are summoned into the Tribune's august presence, where, instead of being executed as they fully expect, they are pardoned and set free, after they have once more solemnly pledged themselves to respect the new government and its chosen representatives. This promise is wrung from them by the force of circumstances; they have no intention of keeping it, and they are no sooner released than they utter dark threats of revenge, which fill the people's hearts with ominous fear, and make them regret the clemency they have just shown.

The next act is played on one of the public squares of Rome, where the people are tumultuously assembled to discuss the secret flight of the barons. They have fled from the city during the night, and, in spite of their recently renewed oaths, are even now preparing to re-enter the city with fire and sword, and to resume their former supremacy. In frantic terror, the people call upon Rienzi to deliver them, declaring that, had he only been firm and executed the nobles, Rome would now have no need to fear their wrath. Adrian, coming upon the spot as they march off toward the Capitol, anxiously deliberates what course he shall pursue, and bitterly reviles fate, which forces him either to bear arms against his own father and kin, or to turn traitor and slay the Tribune, the brother of his fair beloved. While he thus soliloquises in his despair, Rienzi appears on horseback, escorted by the Roman troops, all loudly chanting a battle song, of which the constant refrain is the Tribune's rallying cry, 'Santo Spirito Cavaliere!' They are on their way to the city gates, where the assembled forces of the barons await them, and Adrian, in a last frantic attempt to prevent bloodshed, throws himself in front of Rienzi's horse, imploring the Tribune to allow him to try once more to conciliate the rebel nobles. But Rienzi utterly refuses to yield again to his entreaties, and marches calmly on, accompanied by the people chanting the last verse of their solemn war-song.

The fourth act is played in front of the Lateran church. The battle has taken place. The barons have been repulsed at the cost of great slaughter. But notwithstanding their losses and the death of their leader, the elder Colonna, the nobles have not relinquished all hope of success. What they failed to secure by the force of arms, they now hope to win by intrigue, for they have artfully won not only the Pope, but the Emperor also, to uphold their cause and side with them. The people, who have just learned that the Pope and Emperor have recalled their legates and ambassadors, are awed and frightened. Baroncelli and Cecco, two demagogues, seize this occasion to poison their fickle minds, and blame Rienzi openly for all that has occurred. Their specious reasoning that the Tribune must be very wicked indeed, since the spiritual and temporal authorities alike disapprove of him, is strengthened by the sudden appearance of Adrian, who, wild with grief at his father's death, publicly declares he has vowed to slay the Tribune. The people—who, lacking the strength to uphold their convictions, now hate their leader as vehemently as they once loved and admired him—are about to join Adrian in his passionate cry of 'Down with Rienzi!' when the cardinal and his train suddenly appear, and march into the church, where a grand 'Te Deum' is to be sung to celebrate the victory over the barons.

While the Romans are wavering, and wondering whether they have not made a mistake, and whether the Pope really disapproves of their chief magistrate, Rienzi marches toward the church, accompanied by Irene and his body guard. Adrian, at the sight of his pale beloved, has no longer the courage to execute his purpose and slay her only brother. Just as they are about to enter the church, where they expect to hear the joyful strains of thanksgiving, the cardinal appears at the church door, barring their entrance, and solemnly pronounces the Church's anathema upon the horror-struck Rienzi.

The people all start back and withdraw from him as from one accursed, while Adrian, seizing Irene's hand, seeks to lead her away from her brother. But the brave girl resists her lover's offers and entreaties, and, clinging closely to the unhappy Tribune, she declares she will never forsake him, while he vows he will never relinquish his hope that Rome may eventually recover her wonted freedom, and again shake off the tyrant's yoke.

The fifth and last act is begun in the Capitol, where Rienzi, the enthusiast, is wrapped in prayer, and forgetting himself entirely, fervently implores Divine protection for his misguided people and unhappy city. He has scarcely ended this beautiful prayer when Irene joins him, and, when he once more beseeches her to leave him, she declares she will never forsake him, even though by clinging to him she must renounce her love,—a passion which he has never known. At this declaration, Rienzi in a passionate outburst tells how deeply he has loved and still loves his mistress, Rome, fallen and degraded though she may be. He loves her, although she has broken faith with him, has turned to listen to the blandishments of another, and basely deserted him at the time of his utmost need.

Irene, touched by his grief, bids him not give way to despair, but adjures him to make a last attempt to regain his old ascendency over the minds of the fickle people. As he leaves her to follow her advice, Adrian enters the hall, wildly imploring her to escape while there is yet time, for the infuriated Romans are coming, not only to slay Rienzi, but to burn down the Capitol which has sheltered him.

As she utterly refuses to listen to his entreaties, he vainly seeks to drag her away. It is only when the lurid light of the devouring flames illumines the hall, and when she sinks unconscious to the floor, that he can bear her away from a place fraught with so much danger for them all. Rienzi, in the mean while, has stepped out on the balcony, whence he has made repeated but futile attempts to address the mob. Baroncelli and Cecco, fearing lest he should yet succeed in turning the tide by his marvellous eloquence, drown his voice by discordant cries, fling stones which fall all around his motionless figure like hail, and clamour for more fuel to burn down the Capitol, which they have sworn shall be his funeral pyre. Calmly now Rienzi contemplates their fury and his unavoidable death, and solemnly predicts that they will regret their precipitancy, as the Capitol falls into ruins over the noble head of the Last of the Tribunes.

THE FLYING DUTCHMAN.

After leaving Riga, where he had accepted the position of Music Director, which he filled acceptably for some time, Wagner went to Pillau, where he embarked on a sailing vessel bound for London. He was accompanied by his wife and by a huge Newfoundland dog, and during this journey learned to know the sea, and became familiar with the sound of the sailors' songs, the creaking of the rigging, the whistling of the wind, and the roar and crash of the waves. This journey made a deep impression upon his imagination. He had read Heine's version of the legend of the Flying Dutchman, and questioned the sailors, who told him many similar yarns. He himself subsequently said: 'I shall never forget that voyage; it lasted three weeks and a half, and was rich in disasters. Three times we suffered from the effects of heavy storms. The passage through the Narrows made a wondrous impression on my fancy. The legend of the Flying Dutchman was confirmed by the sailors, and the circumstances gave it a distinct and characteristic colour in my mind.'

One year later, when in Paris, Wagner submitted detailed sketches for this work to the Director of the Opera, to whom Meyerbeer had introduced him. The sketches were accepted, and shortly after the Director expressed a wish to purchase them. Wagner utterly refused at first to give up his claim to the plot, which he had secured from Heine; but, finding that he could not obtain possession of the sketches, which had already been given to Foucher for versification, he accepted the miserable sum of £20, which was all that was offered in compensation. The stolen opera was produced in Paris under the title of 'Le Vaisseau Fantôme,' in 1842, but it was never very successful, and has been entirely eclipsed by Wagner's version. Wagner had not, however, relinquished the idea of writing an opera upon this theme, and he finished the poem, which Spohr has designated as 'a little masterpiece,' as quickly as possible. The score was written at Meudon, near Paris, and completed, with the exception of the overture, in the short space of seven weeks. When offered in Munich and Leipsic the critics pronounced it 'unfit for Germany,' but, upon Meyerbeer's recommendation, it was accepted at Berlin, although no preparations were made for its immediate representation.

'The Flying Dutchman' was first brought out at Dresden in 1843, four years after the idea of this work had first suggested itself to the illustrious composer, who conducted the orchestra in person, while Madame Schröder-Devrient sang the part of Senta. The audience did not receive it very enthusiastically, and, while some of the hearers were deeply moved, the majority were simply astonished. No one at first seemed to appreciate the opera at its full value except Spohr, who in connection with it wrote: 'Der Fliegende Holländer interests me in the highest degree. The opera is imaginative, of noble invention, well written for the voices, immensely difficult, rather overdone as regards instrumentation, but full of novel effects; at the theatre it is sure to prove clear and intelligible.... I have come to the conclusion that among composers for the stage, *pro tem.*, Wagner is the most gifted.'

The legend upon which the whole opera is based is that a Dutch captain once tried to double the Cape of Good Hope in the teeth of a gale, swearing he would accomplish his purpose even if he had to plough the main forever. This rash oath was overheard by Satan, who condemned him to sail until the Judgment Day, unless he could find a woman who would love him faithfully until death. Once in every seven years only did the Devil allow the Dutchman to land, in search of the maiden who might effect his release.

In the first act of the opera, the seven years have just ended, and Daland, a Norwegian captain, has been forced by a tempest to anchor his vessel in a sheltered bay within a few miles of his peaceful home, where Senta, his only daughter, awaits him. All on board are sleeping, and the steersman alone keeps watch over the anchored vessel, singing of the maiden he loves and of the gifts he is bringing her from foreign lands. In the midst of his song, the Flying Dutchman's black-masted vessel with its red sails enters the cove, and casts anchor beside the Norwegian ship, although no one seems aware of its approach.

The Dutchman, who has not noticed the vessel at anchor so near him, springs eagerly ashore, breathing a sigh of relief at being allowed to land once more, although he has but little hope of finding the faithful woman who alone can release him from his frightful doom:—

'The term is past,
And once again are ended the seven long years!
The weary sea casts me upon the land.
Ha! haughty ocean,
A little while, and thou again wilt bear me.
Though thou art changeful,
Unchanging is my doom;
Release, which on the land I seek for,
Never shall I meet with.'

The unhappy wanderer then tells how he has braved the dangers of every sea, sought death on every rock, challenged every pirate, and how vain all his efforts have been to find the death which always eludes him.

Daland, waking from his sound slumbers, suddenly perceives the anchored vessel, and chides the drowsy steersman, who has not warned him of its approach. He is about to signal to the ship to ascertain its name, when he suddenly perceives the Dutchman, whom he questions concerning his home and destination.

The Dutchman answers his questions very briefly, and, upon hearing that Daland's home is very near, eagerly offers untold wealth for permission to linger a few hours by his fireside, and to taste the joys of home.

Amazed at the sight of the treasures spread out before him, Daland not only consents to show hospitality to this strange homeless guest, but even promises, after a little persuasion, to allow him to woo and to win, if he can, the affections of his only daughter, Senta:—

'I give thee here my word.
I mourn thy lot. As thou art bountiful,
Thou showest me thy good and noble heart.
My son I wish thou wert;
And were thy wealth not half as great,
I would not choose another.'

Transported with joy at the mere prospect of winning the love which may compass his salvation, the Flying Dutchman proclaims in song his mingled rapture and relief, and while he sings the storm clouds break, and the sun again shines forth over the mysteriously calmed sea. The opportunity is immediately seized by the Norwegian captain, who, bidding the Dutchman follow him closely, bids the sailors raise the anchor, and sails out of the little harbour to the merry accompaniment of a nautical chorus:—

'Through thunder and storm from distant seas,
My maiden, come I near;
Over towering waves, with southern breeze,
My maiden, am I here.
My maiden, were there no south wind,
I never could come to thee:
O fair south wind, to me be kind!
My maiden, she longs for me.
   Hoho! Halloho!'

The next scene represents a room in Daland's house. The rough walls are covered with maps and charts, and on the farther partition there is a striking portrait of a pale, melancholy looking man, who wears a dark beard and a foreign dress.

The air is resonant with the continual hum of the whirling spinning-wheels, for the maidens are all working diligently under the direction of Maria, the housekeeper, and soon begin their usual spinning chorus. Their hands and feet work busily while two verses of the song are sung, and all are remarkably diligent except Senta, who sits with her hands in her lap, gazing in rapt attention at the portrait of the Flying Dutchman, whose mournful fate has touched her tender heart, and whose haunting eyes have made her indulge in many a long day-dream. Roused from her abstraction by the chiding voice of Mary, and by her companions, who twit her with having fallen in love with a shadow instead of thinking only of her lover Erik, the hunter, Senta resumes her work, and to still their chatter sings them the ballad of the Flying Dutchman. When she has described his aimless wanderings and his mournful doom, which naught can change until he finds a maiden who will pledge him her entire faith, the girls mockingly interrupt her to inquire whether she would have the courage to love an outcast and to follow a spectral wooer. But when Senta passionately declares she would do it gladly, and ends by fervently praying that he may soon appear to put her love and faith to the test, they are almost as much alarmed as Erik, who enters the room in time to hear this enthusiastic outburst.

Turning to Mary, the housekeeper, he informs her that Daland's ship has just sailed into the harbour in company with another vessel, whose captain and crew he doubtless means to entertain. At these tidings the wheels are all set aside, and the maidens hasten to help prepare the food for the customary feast. Senta alone remains seated by her wheel, and Erik, placing himself beside her, implores her not to leave him for another, but to put an end to his sorrows by promising to become his wife. His eloquent pleading has no effect upon her, however, and when he tries to deride her fancy for the pictured face, and to awaken her pity for him by describing his own sufferings, she scornfully compares them to the Dutchman's unhappy fate:—

'Oh, vaunt it not!
What can thy sorrow be?
Know'st thou the fate of that unhappy man?
Look, canst thou feel the pain, the grief,
With which his gaze on me he bends?
Ah! when I think he has ne'er found relief,
How sharp a pang my bosom rends!'

Erik, beside himself with jealousy, finally tells her that he has had an ominous dream, in which he saw her greet the dark stranger, embrace him tenderly, and even follow him out to sea, where she was lost. But all this pleading only makes Senta more obstinate in her refusal of his attentions, and more eager to behold the object of her romantic attachment, who at that very moment enters the house, following her father, who greets her tenderly. The sudden apparition of the stranger, whose resemblance to the portrait is very striking, robs Senta of all composure, and it is only when her father has gently reproved her for her cold behaviour that she bids him welcome.

Daland then explains to his daughter that his guest is a wanderer and an exile, although well provided with this world's goods, and asks her whether she would be willing to listen to his wooing, and would consent to ratify his conditional promise by giving the stranger her hand:—

'Wilt thou, my child, accord our guest a friendly welcome,
And wilt thou also let him share thy kindly heart?
Give him thy hand, for bridegroom it is thine to call him,
If thou but give consent, to-morrow his thou art.'

Wholly uninfluenced by the description of the stranger's wealth which her father gives her, but entirely won by the Flying Dutchman's timidly expressed hope that she will not refuse him the blessing he has so long and so vainly sought, Senta hesitates no longer, but generously promises to become his wife, whatever fate may await her:—

'Whoe'er thou art, where'er thy curse may lead thee,
And me, when I thy lot mine own have made,—
Whate'er the fate which I with thee may share in,
My father's will by me shall be obeyed.'

This promise at first fills the heart of the Flying Dutchman with the utmost rapture, for he is thinking only of himself, and of his release from the curse, but soon he begins to love the innocent maiden through whom alone he can find rest. Then he also remembers that, if she fail, she too will be accursed, and, instead of urging her as before, he now tries to dissuade her from becoming his wife by depicting life at his side in the most unenticing colours, and by warning her that she must die if her faith should waver. Senta, undeterred by all these statements, and eager if necessary to sacrifice herself for her beloved, again offers to follow him, and once more a rapturous thrill passes through his heart:—

'SENTA.
Here is my hand! I will not rue,
But e'en to death will I be true.
　　THE DUTCHMAN.
She gives her hand! I conquer you,
Dread powers of Hell, while she is true.'

Daland returns into the room in time to see that they have agreed to marry, and proposes that their wedding should take place immediately, and be celebrated at the same time as the feast which he generally gives all his sailors at the end of a happy journey.

The third act of this opera represents both ships riding at anchor in a rocky bay, near which rises Daland's picturesque Norwegian cottage. All is life and animation on board the Norwegian vessel, where the sailors are dancing and singing in chorus, but the black-masted ship appears deserted, and is as quiet as the tomb.

When the sailors have ended their chorus, the pretty peasant girls come trooping down to the shore, bringing food and drink for both crews, which they hail from the shore. The Norwegian sailors promptly respond to their call, and, hastening ashore, they receive their share of the feast; but the phantom vessel remains as lifeless as before. In vain the girls offer the provisions they have brought, in vain the other crew taunt the sleepers, there is no answer given. The provisions are then all bestowed upon the Norwegians, who eat and drink most heartily ere they resume their merry chorus. Suddenly, however, the Dutch sailors rouse themselves, appear on deck, and prepare to depart, while singing about their captain, who has once more gone ashore in search of the faithful wife who alone can save him. Blue flames hover over the phantom ship, and the sound of a coming storm is borne upon the breeze. The Norwegian sailors sing louder than ever to drown this ominous sound, but they are soon too alarmed to sing, and hasten into their cabins making the sign of the cross, which evokes a burst of demoniac laughter from the phantom crew.

The storm and lights subside as quickly and mysteriously as they appeared, and all is quiet once more as Senta comes down to the shore. Erik, meeting her, implores her to listen to his wooing, which once found favour, and to forget the stranger whom her father has induced her to accept on such short notice. Senta listens patiently to his plea, which does not in the least shake her faith in her new lover, or change her resolution to live and die for him alone. But the Dutchman, appearing suddenly, mistakes her patience for regret, and, almost frantic with love and despair, he bids her a passionate farewell and rushes off toward his ship.

'To sea! To sea till time is ended!
Thy sacred promise be forgot,
Thy sacred promise and my fate!
Farewell! I wish not to destroy thee!'

But Senta has not ceased to love him. She runs after him, imploring him to remain with her, protesting her fidelity and renewing her vows in spite of Erik's passionate efforts to prevent her from doing so. The Flying Dutchman at first refuses to listen to her words, and rapidly gives his orders for departure. She is about to embark, when he suddenly turns toward her and declares that he is accursed, and that she has saved herself, by timely withdrawal, from the doom which awaits all those who fail to keep their troth:—

'Now hear, and learn the fate from which thou wilt be saved:
Condemned am I to bear a frightful fortune,—
Ten times would death appear a brighter lot.
A woman's hand alone the curse can lighten,
If she will love me, and till death be true.
Still to be faithful thou hast vowed,
Yet has not God thy promise?
This rescues thee; for know, unhappy, what a fate is theirs
Who break the troth which they to me have plighted:
Endless damnation is their doom!
Victims untold have fallen 'neath this curse through me.
Yet, Senta, thou shalt escape.
Farewell! All hope is fled forevermore.'

But Senta has known from the very beginning who this dark wooer was, and is so intent upon saving him from his fate that she fears no danger for herself.

Passionately she clings to him, protesting her affection, and when he looses her, and Erik would fain detain her by force, she struggles frantically to follow him.

Erik's cry brings Daland, Mary, and the Chorus to the rescue, and they too strive to restrain Senta, when they hear the stranger proclaim from the deck of his phantom ship that he is the Scourge of the Sea,—the Flying Dutchman. The vessel sails away from the harbour. Senta escapes from her friends, and rushes to a projecting cliff, whence she casts herself recklessly into the seething waves, intent only upon showing her love and saving him, and thereby proving herself faithful unto death:—

'Praise thou thine angel for what he saith;
Here stand I, faithful, yea, till death!'

As Senta sinks beneath the waves the phantom vessel vanishes also, and as the storm abates and the rosy evening clouds appear in the west the transfigured forms of Senta and the Flying Dutchman hover for a moment over the wreck, and, rising slowly, float upward and out of sight, embracing each other, for her faithful love has indeed accomplished his salvation, and his spirit, may now be at rest.

TANNHÄUSER.

In 1829, when Wagner was only sixteen years of age, he first became acquainted, through Hoffmann's novels, with the story of the mastersingers of Nürnberg, and with the mediæval legend of Tannhäuser, as versified by Ludwig Tieck. The 'mystical coquetry and frivolous catholicism' of this modern poem repelled him, and it was not until twelve years later, when he chanced upon a popular version of the same story, that he was struck by its dramatic possibilities. A chance mention of the Sängerkrieg of the Wartburg in this version made him trace the legend as far back as possible, and in doing so he came across an old poem of Lohengrin, and read Eschenbach's 'Titurel' and 'Parzival,' which were to serve as basis for two other great operas. The sketch of the opera of 'Tannhäuser' was completed in 1842, at Teplitz, during an excursion in the Bohemian mountains; but the whole score was not finished until three years later. Wagner had gone over it all so carefully that it was printed without much revision, and he had even written the piano score, which was sent to Berlin in 1845 and appeared in the same year that the opera was produced at Dresden.

Madame Schröder-Devrient, whom Wagner had in his mind in writing the part of Venus, sang that rôle, but, in spite of all her talent, the first performance was not a success. She wrote to Wagner concerning it, and said, 'You are a man of genius, but you write such eccentric stuff it is hardly possible to sing it.' The public in general, accustomed to light operas with happy endings, was dismayed at the sad and tragical termination, and, while some of the best musical authorities of the day applauded, others criticised the work unsparingly. Schumann alone seems to have realised the force of the author's new style, for he wrote, 'On the whole, Wagner may become of great importance and significance to the stage,'—a doubtful prediction which was only triumphantly verified many years afterward. Like many of the mediæval legends, the story of Tannhäuser is connected with the ancient Teutonic religion, which declared that Holda, the Northern Venus, had set up her enchanted abode in the hollow mountain known as the Hörselberg, where she entertained her devotees with all the pleasures of love. When the missionaries came preaching Christianity, they diligently taught the people that all these heathen divinities were demons, and although Holda and her court were not forgotten, she became a type of sensual love. Tannhäuser, a minstrel of note, who has won many prizes for his songs, hearing of the wondrous underground palace and of its manifold charm, voluntarily enters the mountain, and abandons himself to the fair goddess's wiles. Here he spends a whole year in her company, surrounded by her train of loves and nymphs, yielding to all her enchantments, which at first intoxicate his poetic and beauty loving soul.

But at last the sensual pleasures in which he has been steeped begin to pall upon his jaded senses. He longs to tear himself away from the enchantress, and to return to the mingled pleasure and pain of earth.

The first scene of the opera represents the charmed grotto where Venus gently seeks to beguile the discontented knight, while nymphs, loves, bacchantes, and lovers whirl about in the graceful mazes of the dance, or pose in charming attitudes. Seeing Tannhäuser's abstraction and evident sadness, Venus artfully questions him, and when he confesses his homesickness, and his intense longing to revisit the earth, she again tries to dazzle him, and cast a glamour over all his senses, so as to make him utterly oblivious of all but her.

Temporarily intoxicated by her charms, Tannhäuser, when called upon to tune his lyre, bursts forth into a song extolling her beauty and fascination; but even before the lay is ended the longing to depart again seizes him, and he passionately entreats her to release him from her thrall:—

"Tis freedom I must win or die,—
For freedom I can all defy;
To strife or glory forth I go,
Come life or death, come joy or woe,
No more in bondage will I sigh!
O queen, beloved goddess, let me fly!'

Thus adjured, and seeing her power is temporarily ended, Venus haughtily dismisses her slave, warning him that he returns to earth in vain, as he has forfeited all chance of salvation by lingering with her, and bidding him return without fear when the intolerance of man has made him weary of life upon earth.

A sudden change of scene occurs. At a sign from Venus, the grotto and its voluptuous figures disappear; the roseate light makes way for the glaring sunshine, and Tannhäuser, who has not moved, suddenly finds himself upon the hillside, near the highroad and the shrine of the Virgin, and within sight of the Wartburg castle, where he formerly dwelt and won many a prize for his beautiful songs. The summer silence is at first broken only by the soft notes of a shepherd singing a popular ballad about Holda, the Northern Venus, who issues yearly from the mountain to herald the spring, but as he ceases a band of pilgrims slowly comes into view. These holy wanderers are all clad in penitential robes, and, as they slowly wend their way down the hill and past the shrine, they chant a psalm praying for the forgiveness of their sins. The shepherd calls to them asking them to pray for him in Rome, and, as they pass out of sight, still singing, Tannhäuser, overcome with remorse for his misspent years, sinks down on his knees before the Virgin's shrine, humbly imploring forgiveness for his sins:—

'Oh, see my heart by grief oppressed!
I faint, I sink beneath the burden!
Nor will I cease, nor will I rest,
Till heavenly mercy grants me pardon.'

While he is still kneeling there, absorbed in prayer, the Landgrave and his minstrel knights appear in hunting costume. Their attention is attracted by the bowed figure of the knight, and when he raises his head they recognise him as their former companion. Some of the minstrels, jealous of his past triumphs, would fain regard him as their foe, but, influenced by one of their number, Wolfram von Eschenbach, they welcome him kindly and ask him where he has been. Tannhäuser, only partly roused from his half lethargic state, dreamily answers that he has long been tarrying in a land where he found neither peace nor rest, and in answer to their invitation to join them in the Wartburg declares he cannot stay, but must wander on forever. Wolfram, seeing him about to depart once more, then reminds him of Elizabeth, the fair chatelaine of the Wartburg, and when he sees that, although Tannhäuser trembles at the mere sound of the name of the maiden he once loved, he will nevertheless depart, he asks and obtains the Landgrave's permission to reveal a long kept secret.

Wolfram himself has long loved the fair Elizabeth, but such is his unselfish devotion that he would fain see her happy even with a rival. To win the light back to her eyes and the smile to her lips, he now tells Tannhäuser how she has drooped ever since he went away, and generously confesses that she took pleasure in his music only, and has persistently avoided the minstrel hall since his departure. His eloquent pleading touches Tannhäuser's reawakening heart, and he finally consents to accompany the Landgrave and his minstrels back to the Wartburg. Hither they now make their way on foot and on horseback, singing a triumphal chorus:—

'He doth return, no more to wander;
Our loved and lost is ours again.
All praise and thanks to those we render
Who could persuade, and not in vain.
Now let your harps indite a measure
Of all that hero's hand may dare,
Of all that poet's heart can pleasure,
Before the fairest of the fair.'

The second act is played in the great hall of the Wartburg castle, which is festively decorated, for the minstrels are again to contend for the prize of song, a laurel wreath which will again be bestowed as of yore by the fair hands of the beloved Princess Elizabeth. As the curtain rises she is alone in the hall, no longer pale and wan, but radiant with happiness, for she knows that Tannhäuser, her lover, has returned, and she momentarily expects him to appear. While she is greeting the well known hall, the scene of her lover's former triumphs, with a rapturous little outburst of song, the door suddenly opens and Wolfram appears, leading the penitent Tannhäuser, who rushes forward and falls at Elizabeth's feet, while his friend discreetly withdraws. Elizabeth would fain raise the knight, telling him it is unbecoming for him to assume so humble an attitude beneath the roof where he has triumphed over all rivals, and she tenderly asks where he has lingered so long. Tannhäuser, ashamed of the past, and absorbed in the present, declares that he has been far away, in the land of oblivion, where he has forgotten all save her alone:—

'Far away in strange and distant regions,
And between yesterday and to-day oblivion's veil hath fallen.
Every remembrance hath forever vanished,
Save one thing only, rising from the darkness,—
That I then dared not hope I should behold thee,
Nor ever raise mine eyes to thy perfection.'

Elizabeth is so happy to see him once more, so ready to forgive him at the very first word of repentance, that Tannhäuser cannot but see how dearly she loves him, and they soon unite in a duet of complete bliss, rejoicing openly over their reunion, and vowing to love each other forever, and never to part again.

The Landgrave appears just as their song is ended, to congratulate Elizabeth upon having at last left her seclusion and honoured the minstrels with her presence. In conclusion, he declares that, as all the contestants know she will be there to bestow the prize, the rivalry will be greater than ever. He is interrupted in this speech, however, by the entrance of knights and nobles, who file in singing a chorus in praise of the noble hall, and of Hermann, Landgrave of Thuringia, the patron of song, whom they repeatedly cheer. When they have all taken their appointed places, the Landgrave, rising in his seat, addresses them, bidding them welcome, reminding them of the high aims of their art, and telling them that, while the theme he is about to propose for their lays is love, the princess herself will bestow as prize whatever the winner may ask:—

'Therefore hear now the theme you all shall sing.
Say, what is love? by what signs shall we know it?
This be your theme. Whoso most nobly this can tell,
Him shall the princess give the prize.
He may demand the fairest guerdon:
I vouch that whatsoe'er he ask is granted.
Up, then, arouse ye! sing, O gallant minstrels!
Attune your harps to love. Great is the prize,'

At the summons of the heralds, Wolfram von Eschenbach first takes up the strain, and as for him love is an ardent desire to see the loved one happy, a longing to sacrifice himself if need be, and an attitude of worshipful devotion, he naturally sings an exalted strain. It finds favour with all his hearers,—with all except Tannhäuser, who, having tasted of the passionate joys of unholy love, cannot understand the purity of Wolfram's lay, which he stigmatises as cold and unsatisfactory.

In his turn, he now attunes his harp to love, and sings a voluptuous strain, which not only contrasts oddly with Wolfram's performance, but shows love merely as a passion, a gratification of the senses. The minstrels, jealous for their art, indignantly interrupt him, and one even challenges Tannhäuser to mortal combat:—

> 'To mortal combat I defy thee!
> Shameless blasphemer, draw thy sword!
> As brother henceforth we deny thee:
> Thy words profane too long we've heard!
> If I of love divine have spoken,
> Its glorious spell shall be unbroken
> Strength'ning in valour, sword and heart,
> Altho' from life this hour I part.
> For womanhood and noble honour
> Through death and danger I would go;
> But for the cheap delights that won thee
> I scorn them as worth not one blow!'

This minstrel's sentiments are loudly echoed by all the knights present, who, having been trained in the school of chivalry, have an exalted conception of love, hold all women in high honour, and deeply resent the attempt just made to degrade them. Tannhäuser, whose once pure and noble nature has been perverted and degraded by the year spent with Venus, cannot longer understand the exalted pleasures of true love, even though he has just won the heart of a peerless and spotless maiden, and when Wolfram, hoping to allay the strife, again resumes his former strain, he impatiently interrupts him.

Recklessly now, and entirely wrapped up in the recollection of the unholy pleasures of the past, Tannhäuser exalts the goddess of Love, with whom he has revelled in bliss, and boldly reveals the fact that he has been tarrying with her in her subterranean grove.

This confession fills the hearts of all present with nameless terror, for the priests have taught them that the heathen deities are demons disguised. The minstrels one and all fall upon Tannhäuser, who is saved from immediate death at their hands only by the prompt intervention of Elizabeth.

Broken-hearted, for now she knows the utter unworthiness of the man to whom she has given her heart, yet loving him still and hoping he may in time win forgiveness for his sin, she pleads so eloquently for him that all fall back. The Landgrave, addressing him, then solemnly bids him repent, and join the pilgrims on their way to Rome, where perchance the Pope may grant him absolution for his sin:—

> 'One path alone can save thee from perdition,
> From everlasting woe,—by earth abandon'd,
> One way is left: that way thou now shalt know.
> A band of pilgrims now assembled
> From every part of my domain;

This morn the elders went before them,
The rest yet in the vale remain.
'Tis not for crimes like thine they tremble,
And leave their country, friends and home,—
Desire for heav'nly grace is o'er them:
They seek the sacred shrine at Rome.'

    Urged to depart by the Landgrave, knights, nobles, and even by the pale and sorrowful Elizabeth, Tannhäuser eagerly acquiesces, for now that the sudden spell of sensuous love has departed, he ardently longs to free his soul from the burden of sin. The pilgrims' chant again falls upon his ear, and, sobered and repentant, Tannhäuser joins them to journey on foot to Rome, kneeling at every shrine by the way, and devoutly praying for the forgiveness and ultimate absolution of his sins.

    When the curtain rises upon the third and last act of this opera, one whole year has slowly passed, during which no tidings of the pilgrims have been received. It is now time for their return, and they are daily expected by their friends, who have ardently been praying that they may come home, shrived and happy, to spend the remainder of their lives at home in peace. No one has prayed as fervently as the fair Elizabeth, who, forgetting her wonted splendour, has daily wended her way down the hillside, to kneel on the rude stones in front of the Virgin's wayside shrine. There she has daily prayed for Tannhäuser's happy return, and there she kneels absorbed in prayer when Wolfram comes down the path as usual. He has not forgotten his love for her, which is as deep and self-sacrificing as ever, so he too prays that her lover may soon return from Rome, entirely absolved, and wipe away her constant tears. Elizabeth is suddenly roused from her devotions by the distant chant of the returning pilgrims. They sing of sins forgiven, and of the peace won by their long, painful journey to Rome. Singing thus they slowly file past Wolfram and Elizabeth, who eagerly scan every face in search of one whom they cannot discover.

    When all have passed by, Elizabeth, realising that she will see her beloved no more, sinks slowly down on her knees, and, raising her despairing eyes to the image of the Virgin. Then she solemnly dedicates the remainder of her life to her exclusive service, in the hope that Tannhäuser may yet be forgiven, and prays that death may soon come to ease her pain and bring her heart eternal peace:—

'O blessed Virgin, hear my prayer!
Thou star of glory, look on me!
Here in the dust I bend before thee,
Now from this earth oh set me free!
Let me, a maiden, pure and white,
Enter into thy kingdom bright!
If vain desires and earthly longing
Have turn'd my heart from thee away,
The sinful hopes within me thronging

Before thy blessed feet I lay.
I'll wrestle with the love I cherish'd,
Until in death its flame hath perish'd.
If of my sin thou wilt not shrive me,
Yet in this hour, oh grant thy aid!
Till thy eternal peace thou give me,
I vow to live and die thy maid.
And on thy bounty I will call,
That heav'nly grace on him may fall.'

This prayer ended, the broken-hearted Elizabeth slowly totters away, while Wolfram von Eschenbach, who has seen by her pallid face and wasted frame that the death she prays for will not tarry long, sorrowfully realises at last that all his love can save her no pang.

When the evening shadows have fallen, and the stars illumine the sky, he is still lingering by the holy shrine where Elizabeth has breathed her last prayer. The silence of the night is suddenly broken by the sound of his harp, as he gives vent to his sorrow by an invocation to the stars, among which his lady-love is going to dwell ere-long, and as he sings the last notes a pilgrim slowly draws near. Wolfram does not at first recognise his old friend and rival Tannhäuser in this dejected, foot-sore traveller; but when he sees the worn face he anxiously inquires whether he has been absolved, and warns him against venturing within the precincts of the Wartburg unless he has received Papal pardon for his sins.

Tannhäuser, instead of answering this query, merely asks him to point out the path, which he once found so easily, the path leading to the Venus hill, and only when Wolfram renews his questions does he vouchsafe him a brief account of his journey to Rome. He tells how he trod the roughest roads barefooted, how he journeyed through heat and cold, eschewing all comforts and alleviation of his hard lot, how he knelt penitently before every shrine, and how fervently he prayed for the forgiveness of the sin which had darkened not only his life but that of his beloved. Then, in faltering tones, he relates how the Pope shrank from him upon hearing that he had sojourned for a year in the Venus hill, and how sternly he declared there could be no more hope of pardon for such a sin than to see his withered staff blossom and bear leaves:—

'If thou hast shar'd the joys of Hell,
If thou unholy flames hast nurs'd
That in the hill of Venus dwell,
Thou art for evermore accurs'd!
And as this barren staff I hold
Ne'er will put forth a flower or leaf,
Thus shalt thou never more behold
Salvation or thy sin's relief.'

Tannhäuser now passionately describes his utter despair, after hearing this awful verdict, his weary homeward journey, and his firm determination, since he is utterly debarred from ever seeing Elizabeth again, either in this world or in the next, to hasten back to the hill of Venus, where he can at least deaden his remorse with pleasure, and steep his sinful soul in sensual love. In vain Wolfram pleads with him not to give up all hope of ultimate salvation, and still to repent of his former sin; he insists upon returning to the enchantress who warned him of the intolerance of man, and whom he now calls upon to guide his steps to the entrance of her abode.

This invocation does not remain unheard by the fair goddess of beauty. She appears in the distance with her shadowy train, singing her old alluring song, and welcoming him back to her realm. Tannhäuser is about to obey her beckoning hand, and to hasten after her in the direction of the Hörselberg, when the sound of a funeral chant falls upon his ear. A long procession is slowly winding down the hill. The mourners are carrying the body of the fair Elizabeth, who has died of grief, to its last resting place.

While Tannhäuser, forgetting all else, is gazing spellbound at the waxen features of his beloved, thus slowly borne down the hill, Wolfram tells him how the pure maiden interceded for him in her last prayer on earth, and declares that he knows her innocent soul is now pleading for his forgiveness at the foot of the heavenly throne. This hope of salvation brings such relief to Tannhäuser's tormented heart, that he turns his back upon Venus, who, realising her prey has escaped, suddenly vanishes in the Hörselberg with all her demon train.

Kneeling by Elizabeth's bier, Tannhäuser fervently prays for forgiveness, until the bystanders, touched by his remorse, assure him that he will be forgiven,—an assurance which is confirmed as he breathes his last, by the arrival of the Pope's messenger. He appears, bearing the withered staff, which has miraculously budded and has burst forth into blossoms and leaves:—

'The Lord himself now thy bondage hath riven. Go, enter in with the blest in His heaven.'

LOHENGRIN.

During a summer vacation at Teplitz in Bohemia, in 1845, Wagner wrote the first sketch of the opera of 'Lohengrin.' The poem was written at Dresden in 1845, but the score was finished only in 1848. The opera was first performed at Weimar in 1850, under the leadership of Liszt, who was greatly interested in it, and determined to make it a success.

The poet composer had taken the idea for this poem from a mediæval legend, based upon the old Greek myth of Cupid and Psyche. Its poetical and musical possibilities immediately struck him, and when the opera was first played to an audience composed of musical and literary people from all parts of Europe, whom Liszt had invited to be present, it produced 'a powerful impression.' From the memorable night of its first performance 'dates the success of the Wagner movement in Germany.' During the next nine years this opera was given in fourteen different cities, and Wagner, who was then a political exile, is reported to have sadly remarked, 'I shall soon be the only German who has not heard Lohengrin.' It was in 1861, eleven years after its first performance, that he finally heard it for the first time in Vienna.

This opera won for Wagner not only lasting fame, but also the enthusiastic admiration of the young Ludwig of Bavaria. Such was the impression this work made upon the young prince, who first heard it when he was only sixteen, that he resolved to do all in his power to help the composer. Three years later he succeeded to the throne of Bavaria as Ludwig II., and one of the first independent acts of his reign was to send a messenger to invite the master to come and dwell at his court, and to assure him a yearly pension from his private purse. The young king was so infatuated with the story of 'Lohengrin' that he not only had his residence decorated with paintings and statues representing different episodes of the opera, but used also to sail about his lake, dressed in the Swan Knight's costume, in a boat drawn by ingeniously contrived mechanical swans. The story of this opera is as follows:—

Henry I., the Fowler, Emperor of Germany, about to make war against the Hungarians who threaten to invade his realm, comes to Antwerp to collect his troops, and to remind all the noblemen of Brabant of their allegiance to him.

The opera opens with the trumpet call of the heralds, and by Henry's speech to the assembled noblemen, who enthusiastically promise him the support of their oft-tried arms. The king, who is pleased with their readiness to serve him, then informs them that he has heard rumours of trouble in their midst, and that by right of his office as high justice of the realm he would fain bring peace among them. He therefore summons Frederick of Telramund, the guardian of the dukedom of Brabant, to state the cause of dissension. This nobleman relates how the dying Duke of Brabant confided his children, Elsa and Godfrey, to his care, how tenderly he watched over them, and how much sorrow he felt when the young heir, having gone out in the forest to walk with his sister one day, failed to return. Frederick of Telramund then goes on, and tells how he could not but suspect Elsa of her brother's murder. He had therefore renounced her hand, which he had once hoped to win, had married Ortrud, daughter of Radbod, the heathen king and former possessor of all this tract of land, which he now claims as his own by right of inheritance.

The people at first refuse to believe his dark accusation against Elsa; but when Frederick declares she murdered her brother so as to become sole mistress of the duchy, and to bestow it upon some unworthy lover, the king sends for the maiden, and, hanging his shield upon an oak, declares he will not depart until he has tried this cause:—

'HERALD.
Now shall the cause be tried as ancient use requires.
KING.
Never again my shield to wear
Till judgment is pronounced, I swear.'

The people receive this decree with joy, and the men, drawing their swords, thrust them into the ground as they form a circle around the king. These preparations for a solemn court of justice are scarcely ended when Elsa appears, all in white, and attended by her ladies, who stand in the background while she timidly advances and stands before the king. Her youth, beauty, and apparent innocence produce a great effect, not only upon the bystanders, but also upon the king, who gently begins to question her.

But, instead of answering him, the fair maiden merely bows and wrings her hands, exclaiming, 'My hapless brother!' until the king implores her to confide in him. Suddenly her tongue is loosened, and she begins to sing, as if in a trance, of a vision with which she has been favoured, wherein a handsome knight had been sent by Heaven to become her champion:—

'I saw in splendour shining
A knight of glorious mien,
On me his eye inclining
With tranquil gaze serene;
A horn of gold beside him,
He leant upon his sword.
Thus when I erst espied him
'Mid clouds of light he soared;
His words so low and tender
Brought life renewed to me.
My guardian, my defender,
Thou shalt my guardian be.'

These words and the maiden's rapt and innocent look are so impressive, that the king and people utterly refuse to believe the maiden guilty of crime, until Frederick of Telramund boldly offers to prove the truth of his assertion by fighting against any champion whom she may choose. Elsa accepts this proposal gladly, for she hopes her heaven-sent champion may appear. The lists are immediately prepared, while the herald calls aloud:—

'He who in right of Heaven comes here to fight For Elsa of Brabant, step forth at once.'

The first call remains unanswered; but, at Elsa's request, the king commands a second to be made, while she sinks on her knees and ardently begins praying for her champion's appearance. Her prayer is scarcely ended when the men along the bank become aware of the approach of a snowy swan, drawing a little skiff, in which a handsome young knight in full armour stands erect.

Amid the general silence of the amazed spectators, Lohengrin, the Swan Knight, springs ashore, and, turning to his swan, dismisses it in a beautiful song, one of the gems of this opera:—

'I give thee thanks, my faithful swan.
Turn thee again and breast the tide;
Return unto that land of dawn
Where joyous we did long abide.
Well thy appointed task is done.
Farewell, my trusty swan.'

Then, while the swan slowly sails down the river and out of sight, the Swan Knight announces to the king that he has come as Elsa's champion, and, turning to her, asks whether she will be his wife if he proves victorious. Elsa gladly promises him her hand, nor does she even offer to withdraw this promise when he tells her that she must trust him entirely, and never ask who he is or whence he comes:—

'Say, dost thou understand me?
Never, as thou dost love me,
Aught shall to question move thee
From whence to thee I came,
Or what my race and name.'

Elsa faithfully promises to remember all these injunctions, and bids him do battle for her, whereupon he challenges Telramund, with whom he begins fighting at a given signal. The Swan Knight soon defeats his enemy, who is thus convicted of perjury by the judgment of God, but he magnanimously refuses to take his life.

Then, turning to Elsa, who thanks him passionately for saving her, he clasps her in his arms, while Telramund and Ortrud, his wife, bewail their disgrace, for, according to the law of the land, they are doomed to poverty and exile. Their sorrow, however, is quite unheeded by the enthusiastic spectators, who set Elsa and Lohengrin upon their shields, and then bear them off in triumph, to the glad accompaniment of martial strains:—

'CHORUS.

> We sing to thee,—we praise thee,
> To highest honour raise thee.
> Stranger, we here greet thee delighted.
> Wrong thou hast righted;
> We gladly greet thee here.
> Thee, thee we sing alone. Thy name shall live in story.
> Oh, never will be one to rival thee in glory!'

It is night when the curtain rises upon the second act; the knights are still revelling in the part of the palace they occupy, while the women's apartments are dark and still. The street is deserted, and on the steps of the cathedral sit Frederick and Ortrud, who have been despoiled of their rich garments, and are now clad like beggars.

Frederick, who feels his disgrace, bitterly reproaches his wife for having blasted his career, and seeks to induce her to depart with him ere day breaks; but Ortrud refuses to go. She is not yet conquered, and passionately bids him rouse himself, and listen to her plan, if he would recover his honour, retrieve his fortunes, and avenge himself for his public defeat. She first persuades him that the Swan Knight won the victory by magic arts only, which was an unpardonable offence, and then declares that, if Elsa could only be prevailed upon to disobey her champion's injunctions and ask his name, the spell which protects him would soon be broken, and he would soon become their prey.

Telramund, overjoyed at the prospect of wiping out his disgrace, acquiesces eagerly, and as Elsa just then appears at her window and softly apostrophises the evening breeze, Ortrud creeps out of the shadow and timidly addresses her, simulating a distress she is far from feeling.

Moved by compassion at the sight of the haughty woman thus laid low, and touched by the pretended repentance she shows, Elsa, whom happiness has made even more tender than usual, eagerly hastens down with two of her attendants, and, opening the door, bids her come in, promising to intercede in her behalf on the morrow. During the subsequent brief conversation Ortrud artfully manages to make Elsa vaguely uneasy, and to sow in her innocent mind the first seeds of suspicion.

Frederick of Telramund, in the mean while, has watched his wife disappear with Elsa, and, hiding in a niche of the old church, he sees the gradual approach of day, and hears the herald proclaiming through the streets the Emperor's ban upon him:—

> 'Our king's august decree through all the lands
> I here make known,—mark well what he commands:
> Beneath a ban he lays Count Telramund
> For tempting Heaven with traitorous intent.
> Whoe'er shall harbour or companion him
> By right shall share his doom with life and limb.'

The unhappy man also hears the herald announce Elsa's coming marriage with the heaven-sent Swan Knight, and grimly tells the bystanders he will soon unmask the traitor. A few minutes later, when he has returned to his hiding place, he sees Elsa appear in bridal array, followed by her women, and by Ortrud, who is very richly clad. But at the church door Ortrud insolently presses in front of Elsa, claiming the right of precedence as her due, and taunting her for marrying a man who has won her by magic arts only, and whose name and origin she does not even know.

This altercation is interrupted by the appearance of the king and his attendants, among whom is the Swan Knight. He hastens to Elsa's side, while the monarch imperiously demands the cause of strife. Lohengrin tenderly questions Elsa, who tells him all. As Ortrud's venomous insinuations have had no apparent effect upon her, he is about to lead her into the church, when Telramund suddenly steps forward, loudly declaring that the Swan Knight overcame him by sorcery, and imploring Elsa not to believe a word he says.

These accusations are, however, dismissed by the king and his men, since Elsa passionately refuses to credit them, and the wedding procession sweeps into the church, followed by the vindictive glances of Telramund and Ortrud,— glances which the trembling Elsa alone seems to perceive.

The third act takes place on that selfsame evening. The festivities are nearly ended, and through opposite doors the wedding procession enters the nuptial chamber to the accompaniment of the well known Bridal Chorus. The attendants soon depart, however, leaving Elsa and Lohengrin to join in a duet of happy married love. Now that they are alone together for the first time, Elsa softly begins chiding her lover for not showing more confidence in her, and revealing who he is. In spite of his tender attempts to turn aside the conversation into a less dangerous channel, she gradually becomes more importunate:—

'Oh, make me glad with thy reliance,
Humble me not that bend so low.
Ne'er shalt thou rue thy dear affiance:
Him that I love, oh let me know!'

Seeing her husband does not yield to her tender pleading, Elsa then redoubles her caresses. Her faint suspicions have taken such firm root, and grow with such rapidity, that she is soon almost wild with suspense. All his attempts to soothe her only seem to excite her more, and suddenly, fancying that she hears the swan boat coming to bear him away from her, she determines to break the magic spell at any cost, as Ortrud cunningly advised her, and demands his name. Just as Lohengrin is gazing upon her in heart-rending but mute reproach, Telramund bursts into the room, with a band of hired assassins, to take his life. A quick motion from Elsa, whose trust returns when she sees her beloved in danger, permits Lohengrin to parry the first blow with his sword, and Frederick of Telramund soon lies dead upon the floor, while his accomplices cringe at Lohengrin's feet imploring his pardon. Day is dawning, and Lohengrin, after caring tenderly for the half-fainting Elsa, bids the would-be assassins bear the corpse into the presence of the king, where he promises to meet Elsa and satisfy all her demands:—

'Bear hence the corpse into the king's judgment hall.
Into the royal presence lead her.
Arrayed as fits so fair a bride;
There all she asks I will concede her,
Nor from her knowledge aught will hide.'

At the last scene the king is again near the river, on his judgment throne, whence he watches the mustering of the troops which are to accompany him to the war, and makes a patriotic speech, to which they gladly respond. Suddenly, however, the four men appear with the corpse of Frederick of Telramund, which they lay at the king's feet, declaring they are obeying the orders of the new lord of Brabant, who will soon come to explain all. Before the king can question further, Elsa appears, pale and drooping, in spite of her bridal array, and just as the king is rallying her at wearing so mournful an expression when her bridegroom is only leaving her for a short time to lead his troops to the fray, the Swan Knight appears, and is enthusiastically welcomed by his men. Sadly he informs them he can no longer lead them on to victory, and declares that he slew Frederick of Telramund in self-defence, a crime for which he is unanimously acquitted.

Then he sadly goes on to relate that Elsa has already broken her promise, and asked the fatal question concerning his name and origin. Proudly he tells them that he has no cause to be ashamed of his lineage, as he is Lohengrin, son of Parsifal, the guardian of the Holy Grail, sent from the temple on Mount Salvatch to save and defend Elsa. The only magic he had used was the power with which the Holy Grail endowed all its defenders, and which never forsook them until they revealed their name:—

'He whom the Grail to be its servant chooses
Is armed henceforth by high invincible might;
All evil craft its power before him loses,
The spirit of the darkness where he dwells takes flight.
Nor will he lose the awful charm it lendeth,
Although he should to distant lands,
When the high cause of virtue he defendeth:
While he's unknown, its spells he still commands.'

Now, he adds, the sacred spell is broken, he can no longer remain, but is forced to return immediately to the Holy Grail, and in confirmation of his word the swan and skiff again appear, sailing up the river. Tenderly the Swan Knight now bids the repentant Elsa farewell, gently resisting her passionate attempts to detain him, and giving her his sword, horn, and ring, which he bids her bestow upon her brother when he returns to protect her. This boon is denied him, because she could not keep faith with him for one short year, at the end of which time he would have been free to reveal his name, and her missing brother would have been restored to her by the power of the Holy Grail.

Placing the fainting Elsa in her women's arms, Lohengrin then goes down toward the swan boat, amid the loud lamentations of all the people, One person only is glad to see him depart, Ortrud, the wife of Telramund, and, thinking he can no longer interfere, she cruelly taunts Elsa with her lack of faith, and confesses that her magic arts and heathen spells have turned the heir of Brabant into the snowy swan which is even now drawing the tiny skiff.

These words, which fill the hearts of Elsa and all the spectators with horror and dismay, are however overheard by Lohengrin, who, accustomed to rely upon Divine aid in every need, sinks upon his knees, and is rapt in silent prayer. Suddenly a beam of heavenly light streams down upon his upturned face, and the white dove of the Holy Grail is seen hovering over his head. Lohengrin, perceiving it, springs to his feet, looses the golden chain which binds the swan to the skiff, and as the snowy bird sinks out of sight a fair young knight in silver armour rises out of the stream. Then all perceive that he is in truth, as Lohengrin proclaims, the missing Godfrey of Brabant, released from bondage by the power of the Holy Grail. Elsa embraces her brother with joy, the king and nobles gladly welcome him, and Ortrud sinks fainting to the ground. Lohengrin, seeing that his beloved has now a protector, springs into the skiff, whose chain is caught by the dove, and rapidly drawn out of sight. As it vanishes, Elsa sinks lifeless to the ground with a last passionate cry of 'My husband!' and all gaze mournfully after him, for they know they will never see Lohengrin, the Swan Knight, again.

TRISTAN AND YSOLDE.

It was in 1854, when still an exile from his native land, that Wagner, weary of his long work, 'The Ring of the Niblungs,' of which only the first two parts were completed, conceived the idea of using the legend of Tristan as basis for a popular opera. Three years later the poem was finished, but the opera was played in Munich only in 1865 for the first time.

The libretto is based on an ancient Celtic myth or legend, which was very popular during the Middle Ages. It was already known in the seventh century, but whether it originally came from Wales or Brittany is a disputed point. It was very widely known, however, and, thanks to the wandering minstrels, it was translated into all the Continental idioms, and became the theme of many poets, even of later times. Since the days when Godfried of Strasburgh wrote his version of the story it has been versified by many others, among whom, in our days, are Matthew Arnold and Swinburne. While the general outline of these various versions remains the same, the legend has undergone many transformations, but Wagner has preserved many of the fundamental ideas of the myth, which is intended to illustrate the overpowering force of passion. The scene was originally laid in Ireland, Cornwall, and French Brittany.

Blanchefleur, sister of King Mark of Cornwall, falls in love with Rivalin, who dies shortly after their union. Withdrawing to her husband's castle in Brittany, Blanchefleur gives birth to a child whom she calls Tristan, as he is the child of sorrow, and, feeling that she cannot live much longer, she intrusts him to the care of her faithful steward, Kurvenal. When the young hero has reached the age of fifteen, his guardian takes him over to Cornwall, where King Mark not only recognises him as his nephew, but also designates him as his heir.

Tristan has been carefully trained, and is so expert in the use of his arms that he soon excites the envy of the courtiers, who are watching for an opportunity to do him harm. The King of Cornwall, having been defeated in battle by the King of Ireland, is obliged to pay him a yearly tribute, which is collected by Morold, a huge giant and a relative of the Irish king. Morold, coming as usual to collect the tribute money, behaves so insolently that Tristan resolves to free the country from thraldom by slaying him. A challenge is given and accepted, and after a terrible combat, such as the mediæval poets love to describe with minute care, the giant falls, after wounding Tristan with his poisoned spear.

The King of Cornwall, instead of sending the wonted tribute to Ireland, now forwards Morold's head, which is piously preserved by Ysolde, the Irish princess, who finds in the wound a fragment of sword by which she hopes to identify the murderer, and avenge her kinsman's death.

Tristan, finding that the skill of all the Cornwall leeches can give him no relief, decides to go to Ireland and claim the help of Ysolde the princess, who, like her mother, is skilled in the art of healing, and knows the antidote for every poison. Fearing, however, lest she may seek to avenge Morold's death, he goes alone, disguised as a harper, and presents himself before her as Tantris, a wandering minstrel.

His precarious condition touches Ysolde's compassionate heart, and she soon uses all her medical science to accomplish his cure, tenderly nursing him back to health. While sitting beside him one day, she idly draws his sword from the scabbard, and her sharp eyes perceive that a piece is missing. Comparing the break in the sword with the fragment in her possession, she is soon convinced that Morold's murderer is at her mercy, and she is about to slay her helpless foe when an imploring glance allays her wrath.

Tristan, having entirely recovered under her care, takes leave of the fair Ysolde, who has entirely lost her heart to him, and returns to Cornwall, where he relates his adventures, and speaks in such glowing terms of Ysolde's beauty and goodness that the courtiers finally prevail upon the king to sue for her hand.

As the courtiers have tried to make the king believe that his nephew would fain keep him single lest he should have an heir, Tristan reluctantly accepts the commission to bear the king's proposals and escort the bride to Cornwall. Ysolde is of course overjoyed at his return, for she fancies he reciprocates her love; but when he makes his errand known, she proudly conceals her grief, and prepares to accompany the embassy to Cornwall, taking with her her faithful nurse, Brangeane.

The Queen of Ireland, another Ysolde, well versed in every magic art, then brews a mighty love potion, which she intrusts to Brangeane's care, bidding her conceal it in her daughter's medicine chest, and administer it to the royal bride and groom on their wedding night, to insure their future happiness by deep mutual love.

Wagner's opera opens on shipboard, where Ysolde lies sullen and motionless under a tent, brooding over her sorrow and nursing her wrath against Tristan, who has further embittered her by treating her with the utmost reserve, and never once approaching her during the whole journey. The call of the pilot floats over the sea, and Ysolde, roused from her abstraction, asks Brangeane where they are. When she learns that the vessel is already within sight of Cornwall, where a new love awaits her, Ysolde gives vent to her despair, and openly regrets that she does not possess her mother's power over the elements, as she would gladly conjure a storm which would engulf the vessel and set her free from a life she abhors.

Brangeane, alarmed at this outburst, vainly tries to comfort her, and as the vessel draws near the land she obeys Ysolde's command and goes to summon Tristan into her presence. Approaching the young hero, who is at the helm, the maid delivers her message, but Tristan refuses to comply, under pretext of best fulfilling his trust by steering the vessel safe to land:—

'In every station
Where I stand
I serve with life and blood
The pearl of womanhood:—
If I the rudder
Rashly left,

Who steer'd then safely the ship
To good King Mark's fair land?'

He further feigns to misunderstand the purport of her message, by assuring her that the discomforts of the journey will soon be over. Kurvenal, his companion, incensed by Brangeane's persistency, then makes a taunting speech to the effect that his master Tristan, the slayer of Morold, is not the vassal of any queen, and the nurse returns to the tent to report her failure. Ysolde, however, has overheard Kurvenal's speech, and when she learns that Tristan refuses to obey her summons, she comments bitterly upon his lack of gratitude for all her tender care, and confides to Brangeane how she spared him when he was ill and at her mercy.

Brangeane vainly tries to make her believe that Tristan has shown his appreciation by wooing her for the king rather than for himself, and when Ysolde murmurs against a loveless marriage, she shows her the magic potion intrusted to her care, which will insure her becoming a loving and beloved wife.

The sight of the medicine chest in which it is secreted unfortunately reminds Ysolde that she too knows the secret of brewing draughts of all kinds, so she prepares a deadly potion, trying all the while to make Brangeane believe that it is a perfectly harmless drug, which will merely make her forget the unhappy past.

While she is thus occupied, Kurvenal suddenly appears to announce that they are about to land, and to bid her prepare to meet the king, who has seen their coming and is wending his way down to the shore to bid her welcome. Ysolde haughtily replies that she will not stir a step until Tristan proffers an apology for his rude behaviour and obeys her summons. After conferring together for a few moments, Tristan and Kurvenal agree that it will be wiser to appease the irate beauty by yielding to her wishes, than to have an *esclandre*, and Tristan prepares to appear before her. Ysolde, in the mean while, has passionately flung herself into Brangeane's arms, fondly bidding her farewell, and telling her to have the magic draught she has prepared all ready to give to Tristan, with whom she means to drink atonement.

While Brangeane, who mistrusts her young mistress, is still pleading with her to forget the past, Tristan respectfully approaches the princess, and when she haughtily reproves him for slighting her commands, he informs her, with much dignity, that he deemed it his duty to keep his distance:—

'Good breeding taught,
 Where I was upbrought,
 That he who brings
 The bride to her lord
 Should stay afar from his trust.'

Ysolde retorts, that, as he is such a rigid observer of etiquette, it would best behoove him to remember that as yet he has not even proffered the usual atonement for shedding the blood of her kin, and that his life is therefore at her disposal. Tristan, seeing she is bent upon revenge, haughtily hands her his sword, telling her that, since Morold was so dear to her, she had better avenge him. Under pretext that King Mark might resent such treatment of his nephew and ambassador, Ysolde refuses to take advantage of his defencelessness, and declares she will consider herself satisfied if he will only pledge her in the usual cup of atonement, which she motions to Brangeane to bring.

The bewildered handmaiden hastily pours a drug into the cup. This she tremblingly brings to her mistress, who, hearing the vessel grate on the pebbly shore, tells Tristan his loathsome task will soon be over, and that he will soon be able to relinquish her to the care of his uncle.

Tristan, suspecting that the contents of the cup are poisonous, nevertheless calmly takes it from her hand and puts it to his lips. But ere he has drunk half the potion, Ysolde snatches it from his grasp and greedily drains the rest. Instead of the ice-cold chill of death which they both expected, Tristan and Ysolde suddenly feel the electric tingle of love rushing madly through all their veins, and, forgetting all else, fall into each other's arms, exchanging passionate vows of undying love.

Brangeane, the only witness of this scene, views with terror the effect of her subterfuge, for, fearing lest her mistress should injure Tristan or herself, she had hastily substituted the love potion intrusted to her care for the poison Ysolde had prepared. While the lovers, clasped in each other's arms, unite in a duet of passionate love, the vessel is made fast to the shore, where the royal bridegroom is waiting, and it is only when Brangeane throws the royal mantle over Ysolde's shoulders, and when Kurvenal bids them step ashore, that the lovers suddenly realise that their brief dream of love is over.

The sudden revulsion from great joy to overwhelming despair proves too much for Ysolde's delicate frame, and she sinks fainting to the deck, just as King Mark appears and the curtain falls upon the first act.

Several days are supposed to have elapsed, when the second act begins. Ysolde after her fainting fit has been conveyed to the king's palace, where she is to dwell alone until her marriage takes place, and where she forgets everything except the passion which she feels for Tristan, who now shares all her feelings. In a hurried private interview the lovers have arranged a code of signals, and it is agreed that as soon as the light in Ysolde's window is extinguished her lover will join her as speedily as possible.

It is a beautiful summer night, and the last echoes of the hunting horn are dying away on the evening breeze, when Ysolde turns to Brangeane, and impatiently bids her put out the light. The terrified nurse refuses to do so, and implores Ysolde not to summon her lover, declaring that she is sure that Melot, one of the king's courtiers, noted her pallor and Tristan's strange embarrassment. In vain she adds that she knows his suspicions have been aroused, and that he is keeping close watch over them both to denounce them should they do anything amiss. Ysolde refuses to believe her.

The princess is so happy that she makes fun of her attendant's forebodings, and, after praising the tender passion she feels, she again bids her put out the light. As Brangeane will not obey this command, Ysolde, too much in love to wait any longer, finally extinguishes the light with her own hand, and bids her nurse go up in the watch-tower and keep a sharp lookout.

Ysolde then hastens to the open door, and gazes anxiously out into the twilighted forest, frantically waving her veil to hasten the coming of her lover, and runs to meet and embrace him when at last he appears.

Blissful in each other's company, Tristan and Ysolde now forget all else, while they exchange passionate vows and declarations of love, bewailing the length of the days which keep them apart, and the shortness of the nights during which they can see each other. In a passionate duet of mutual love and admiration, they also rejoice that, instead of dying together, as Ysolde had planned, they are still able to live and love.

Brangeane, posted in the watch-tower above, repeatedly warns them that they had better part, but her wise advice proves useless, and it is only when she utters a loud cry of alarm that Tristan and Ysolde start apart. Simultaneously almost with Brangeane's cry, Kurvenal rushes upon the scene with drawn sword, imploring his master to fly; but ere this advice can be followed King Mark and the traitor Melot appear, closely followed by all the royal hunting party. Ysolde, overcome with shame at being thus detected with her lover, sinks fainting to the ground, while Tristan, wishing to shield her as much as possible from the scornful glances of these men, stands in front of her with his mantle outspread. He, too, is overwhelmed with shame, and silently bows his head when his uncle bitterly reproves him for betraying him, and robbing him of the bride he had already learned to love. Even the sentence of banishment pronounced upon him seems none too severe, and Tristan, almost broken-hearted at the sight of his uncle's grief, sadly turns to ask Ysolde whether she will share his lot. Shame and discovery have in no wise diminished her affection for him, and when she promises to follow him even to the end of the earth he cannot restrain his joy, and notwithstanding the king's presence he passionately clasps her in his arms:

'Wherever Tristan's home may be,
 That will Ysolde share with thee:
 That she may follow
 And to thee hold,
 The way now shown to Ysold'!'

Melot, enraged at this sight, rushes upon Tristan with drawn sword, and wounds him so sorely that he falls back unconscious in Kurvenal's arms, while Ysolde, clinging to him, faints away as the curtain falls on the second act.

The third act is played in Tristan's ancestral home in Brittany, whither he has been conveyed by Kurvenal, who vainly tries to nurse his wounded master back to health and strength. The sick man is lying under a great linden tree, in death-like lethargy, while Kurvenal anxiously watches for the vessel which he trusts will bring Ysolde from Cornwall. She alone can cure his master's grievous wound, and her presence only can woo him back from the grave into which he seems rapidly sinking.

From time to time Kurvenal interrupts his sad watch beside the pallid sleeper to call to a shepherd piping on the hillside, and to inquire of him whether he descries any signs of the coming sail. Slowly and feebly Tristan at last opens his eyes, gazes dreamily at his attendant and surroundings, and wonderingly inquires how he came thither. Kurvenal gently tells him that he bore him away from Cornwall while wounded and unconscious, and brought him home to recover his health amid the peaceful scenes of his happy youth; but Tristan sadly declares that life has lost all its charms since he has parted from Ysolde. In a sudden return of delirium the wounded hero then fancies he is again in the forest, watching for the light to go out, until Kurvenal tells him that Ysolde will soon be here, as he has sent a ship to Cornwall to bring her safely over the seas.

These tidings fill Tristan's heart with such rapture that he embraces Kurvenal, thanking him brokenly for his lifelong devotion, and bidding him climb up into the watch-tower that he may catch the first glimpse of the coming sail. While Kurvenal is hesitating whether he shall obey this order and leave his helpless patient alone, the shepherd joyfully announces the appearance of the ship. Kurvenal, ascending the tower, reports to his master how it rounds the point, steers past the dangerous rocks, touches the shore, and permits Ysolde to land.

Tristan has feverishly listened to all these reports, and bids Kurvenal hasten down to bring Ysolde to him; then, left alone, he bursts forth into rapturous praise of the happy day which brings his beloved to him once more, and of the deep love which has called him back from the gates of the tomb. His impatience to see Ysolde soon gets the better of his weakness, however, and he struggles to rise from his couch, although the exertion causes his wounds to bleed afresh. Painfully he staggers half across the stage to meet Ysolde, who appears only in time to hear his last passionate utterance of her beloved name, and to catch his dying form in her arms. She does not realise that he has breathed his last, however, and gently tries to woo him back to life, and make him open his eyes. But when all her efforts have failed, and she finds his heart no longer beats beneath her hand, she reproaches him tenderly for leaving her thus alone, and sinks unconscious upon his breast. Kurvenal, standing beside the lovers, speechless with grief, is roused to sudden action by the shepherd's hurried announcement that a second ship has arrived, and that King Mark, Melot, and all his train, are about to appear. Frenzied with grief, and thinking that they have come once more to injure his master, Kurvenal seizes his sword, and, springing to the gate, fights desperately until he has slain Melot, and falls mortally wounded at Tristan's feet.

While the fight is taking place, King Mark and Brangeane, standing without the castle wall, vainly call to him to stay his hand, as they have come with friendly intentions only, and now that he can resist them no longer they all come rushing in. They are horror-struck at the sight of Tristan and Ysolde, both apparently dead; but Brangeane, having discovered that her mistress has only swooned, soon restores her to consciousness. King Mark hastens to assure Ysolde that she and Tristan are both forgiven; for Brangeane having penitently revealed to him the secret of the love potion which she administered, he realises that they could not but yield to its might. Ysolde, however, pays no heed to his words, but, gazing fixedly at Tristan, she mournfully extols his charms and love, until her heart breaks with grief, and she too sinks lifeless to the ground. No restoratives can now avail to recall the life which has flown forever, and King Mark blesses the corpses of the lovers, and of the faithful servant who has expired at their feet, as the curtain falls.

THE MASTER SINGERS OF NUREMBERG.

When Richard Wagner was only sixteen years of age he read with great enthusiasm one of Hoffmann's novels entitled 'Sängerkrieg,' giving a romantic account of the ancient musical contests at the Wartburg in Bavaria. The impression made upon him by this account was first utilised in his opera of 'Tannhäuser,' when his attention was attracted also to the picturesque possibilities of the guilds formed by the burghers.

It was not until 1845, however, that he made definite use of this material, and began the sketch for his only comic opera. The first outline was drawn during a sojourn in the Bohemian mountains, when he felt in an unusually light and festive mood. But the work was soon set aside, and was not resumed until 1862, when it was finished in Paris. The score was then begun, and written almost entirely at Biberich on the Rhine, and Wagner himself conducted the overture for the first time at a concert in Leipzig.

This fragment was very well received and there was an 'enthusiastic demand for a repetition, in which the members of the orchestra took part as much as the audience.' The opera itself, however, was first performed under Von Bülow, in 1868, at Munich. The best singers of the day took the principal parts, and the result of their united efforts was 'a perfect performance; the best that had hitherto been given of any work of the master.'

The opera, at first intended as a comical pendant to 'Tannhäuser,' is, as we have already stated, Wagner's first and only attempt to write in the comic vein, and the text is full of witty and cutting allusions to the thick-headed critics (at whose hands Wagner had suffered so sorely), who sweepingly condemn everything that does not conform to their fixed standard. During all the Middle Ages, and more especially in the middle of the thirteenth century, the quaint old city of Nuremberg was the seat of one of the most noted musical guilds, or German training schools for poets and musicians. The members of this fraternity were all burghers, instead of knights like the Minnesingers, and held different ranks according to their degree of proficiency. They were therefore called singers when they had mastered a certain number of tunes; poets when they could compose verses to a given air; and Master Singers when they could write both words and music on an appointed theme. The musical by-laws of this guild were called 'Tabulatur,' and every candidate was forced to pass an examination, seven mistakes being the maximum allowed by the chief examiner, who bore the title of Marker.

The opera opens in the interior of St. Catharine's church in Nuremberg, where a closing hymn in honour of St. John is being sung. Eva Pogner and her maid, Magdalena, have been present at the service, and are still standing in their pew. But, in spite of her handmaiden's energetic signs and nudges, the young lady pays but little heed to the closing hymn, and turns all her attention upon a handsome young knight, Walther von Stolzenfels, who, as the last note dies away, presses eagerly forward and enters into conversation with her.

To secure a few moments' private interview Eva sends her maid back to the pew, first for her forgotten kerchief, next for a pin which she has lost, and lastly for her prayer-book. During these temporary absences the deeply enamoured youth implores Eva to tell him whether she is still free, and whether her heart and hand are still at her own disposal. Before the agitated girl can answer, the servant comes up, and, overhearing the question, declares that her mistress's hand has already been promised,—a statement which Eva modifies by adding that her future bridegroom is yet to be chosen. As these contradictory answers greatly puzzle Walther, she hurriedly explains that her father, the wealthiest burgher of the town, wishing to show his veneration for music, has promised his fortune and her hand to a Master Singer, the preference being given to the one who will win the prize on the morrow. The only proviso made is that the girl may remain free if the bridegroom does not win her approval, and Eva timidly confesses that she will either marry Walther or remain single all her life. Magdalena, who has been carrying on a lively flirtation of her own with David, the sexton, now suddenly hurries her young mistress off, bidding the knight apply to David if he would learn any more concerning the musical test about to take place, and in the same breath she promises her lover some choice dainties if he will only do all in his power to enlighten and favour her mistress's suitor.

'Let David supply all
The facts of the trial.—
David, my dear, just heed what I say!
You must induce Sir Walther to stay.
The larder I'll sweep,
The best for you keep;
To-morrow rewards shall fall faster
If this young knight is made Master.'

Walther, who has just passionately declared to Eva that he knows he could become both poet and musician for her sweet sake, since her father has vowed never to allow her to marry any but a Master, now listens attentively to David's exposition of the school's rules and regulations. In the mean while the apprentices come filing in, prepare the benches and chairs, arrange the Marker's curtained box, and gayly chaff each other as they join in an impromptu dance.

They only subside when Pogner, Eva's father, enters with Beckmesser, an old widower, the Marker of the guild, who flatters himself he can easily win the prize on the morrow, and would fain make Pogner promise that the victor should receive the maiden's hand without her consent being asked. He fears lest the capricious fair one may yet refuse to marry him, and decides to make sure of her by singing a serenade under her window that very night. But when he sees the handsome young candidate step forward and receive the support of Pogner, (who has already made his acquaintance, and who evidently is inclined to favour him,) the widower looks very glum indeed, and vindictively resolves to prevent his entrance into the guild by fair means or by foul.

Hans Sachs, the poet shoemaker of Nuremberg, and all the other members of the guild, having now appeared, Beckmesser calls the roll, and Pogner repeats his offer to give his fortune and daughter to the winner of the prize on the morrow, and charges the guild to select their candidates for the contest. Of course the very first thing to be done is to examine the new candidate. Walther, when questioned concerning his teachers and method, boldly declares he has learned his art from nature alone, chooses love as his theme for a trial song, and bursts forth into an impassioned and beautiful strain. But as his words and music are strictly original, and therefore cannot be judged by the usual canons, Beckmesser savagely marks down mistake after mistake, and brusquely interrupts the song to declare the singer is 'outsung and outdone.' In proof of this assertion he exhibits his slate, which is covered with bad marks. Hans Sachs, the only member present who has understood the beauty of this original lay, vainly tries to interfere in Walther's behalf, but his efforts only call forth a rude attack on Beckmesser's part, who advises him to reserve his opinions, stick to his last, and finish the pair of shoes which he has promised him for the morrow. Walther is finally allowed to finish his song, but the prejudiced and intolerant citizens of Nuremberg utterly refuse to receive him in their guild, and he rushes out of the hall in despair, for he has lost his best chance to win the hand of his lady love by competing for the prize on the morrow. His departure is a signal for a tumultuous breaking up of the meeting, the apprentices dancing as before, as soon as their masters have departed.

The second act represents one of the tortuous alleys and a long straight street of the quaint old city of Nuremberg. On one side is Hans Sachs's modest shoemaker's shop, on the other the entrance to Pogner's stately dwelling. It is evening, and David, the shoemaker's apprentice, is leisurely putting up the shutters, when his attention is suddenly attracted by Magdalena, who appears with a basket of dainties. She however refuses to give them to him until he tells her the result of the musical examination. When she hears that Walther has failed and has been refused admittance to the guild, she pettishly snatches the basket from his grasp and flounces off in great displeasure. The other apprentices, who in the mean while have slyly drawn near, now make unmerciful fun of David, who stands stupidly in the middle of the street gazing regretfully after her.

This rough play is soon ended by the appearance of Hans Sachs. He orders all the apprentices to bed, and, by a judicious application of his strap, drives David into the house. Quiet has just been restored once more, when Pogner and Eva come sauntering down the street, returning from their customary evening walk, and sit down side by side on the bench in front of their door.

Here Pogner tries to sound his daughter's feelings, and to discover whether she has any preference among the morrow's candidates, reiterating his decision, however, that he will never allow her to marry any one except a man who has publicly won the title of Master Singer. As he cannot ascertain his daughter's feelings, he soon enters the house, while Eva lingers outside watching for Walther's promised visit. She is soon joined by Magdalena, who sorrowfully tells her that Walther has been rejected; but, as she can give no details about the examination, Eva timidly approaches Hans Sachs's window hoping to learn more from him. The cobbler is sitting at work near his window, singing a song of his own composition, and the maiden soon enters into a bantering conversation with her old friend.

In answer to Hans Sachs's questions, she soon confides to him that she cannot endure Beckmesser, and to flatter him into a good humour she archly suggests that, as he too is a widower, he ought to compete for her hand. Hans Sachs, who is far too shrewd not to see through her girlish fencing, now resolves to discover whether she is as indifferent to the young knight, and in order to do so he drops a few careless and contemptuous remarks about him, which drive the young lady away in a very bad temper.

Smiling maliciously at the success of his ruse, the cobbler cheerfully continues his work, while Eva rejoins Magdalena, who informs her that Beckmesser has signified his intention to serenade her that very night. Eva cares naught for the widower's music, and, only intent upon securing a private interview with the handsome young knight, refuses to re-enter the house; so Magdalena leaves her to answer Pogner's call.

A few moments later Walther himself comes slowly down the street; but, in spite of Eva's rapturous welcome, he remains plunged in melancholy, for he has forfeited all hope of winning her on the morrow. The sound of the watchman's horn drives the young people apart, and while Eva vanishes into the house, Walther hides under the shadow of the great linden tree in front of Sachs's house.

His presence has been detected by the shoemaker, who makes no sign, and when the night watchman has gone by, singing the hour and admonishing all good people to go to bed, he perceives a female form glide softly out of the house and join the knight. This female is Eva, who has exchanged garments with Magdalena, and has prevailed upon her to pose at her window during the serenade, while she tries to comfort her beloved.

Crouching in the shade, the lovers now plan to elope that very night, but Hans Sachs overhears their conversation, and when they are about to leave their hiding-place and depart, he flings open his shutter so that a broad beam of light streams across the old street. It makes such a brilliant illumination that it is impossible for any one to pass unseen. This ruse, which proves such a hindrance to the lovers, is equally distasteful to Beckmesser, who has come down the street and has taken his stand near them to tune his lute and begin his serenade. Before he can utter the first note, Hans Sachs, having become aware of his presence also, and maliciously anxious to defeat his plans, lustily entones a noisy ditty about Adam and Eve, hammering his shoes to beat time.

Beckmesser, who has seen Eva's window open, and longs to make himself heard, steps up to the shoemaker's window. In answer to his testy questions why he is at his bench at such an hour, Hans Sachs good-humouredly replies that he must work late to finish the shoes about which he has been twitted in public. At his wit's end to silence the shoemaker and sing his serenade, Beckmesser artfully pretends that he would like to have Sachs's opinion of the song he intends to sing on the morrow, and proposes to let him hear it then. After a little demur the shoemaker consents, upon condition that he may give a tap with his hammer every time he hears a mistake, and thus carry on the double office of marker and of cobbler.

Beckmesser is, however, so angry and agitated that his song is utterly spoiled, and he makes so many mistakes that the cobbler's hammer keeps up an incessant clatter. These irritating sounds make the singer more nervous still, and he sings so loudly and so badly that he rouses the whole neighbourhood, and heads pop out of every window to bid him be still.

David also ventures to peer forth, and, seeing that the serenade is directed to Magdalena, whom he recognises at the window above, his jealous anger knows no bounds. He springs out of the window, and begins belabouring his unlucky rival with a stout cudgel. The Nuremberg apprentices, who are divided up into numerous rival guilds, and who are always quarrelling, seize this occasion to bandy words, which soon result in bringing them all out into the street, where a free fight takes place between the rival factions of journeymen and apprentices.

Magdalena, seeing her beloved David in peril screams aloud, until Pogner, deceived by her apparel, pulls her into the room and closes the window, declaring he must go and see that all is safe. Sachs, who has closed his shutter at the first sounds of the fight, steals out into the street, approaches the young lovers, and, pretending to take Eva for Magdalena, he thrusts her quickly into Pogner's house, and drags Walther into his own dwelling just as the sound of the approaching night watch is heard. As if by magic the brawlers suddenly disappear, the windows close, the lights are extinguished, and as the watchman turns the corner the street has resumed its wonted peaceful aspect.

The third act opens on the morrow, in Hans Sachs's shop, where the cobbler is absorbed in reading and oblivious of the presence of his apprentice David, who comes sneaking in with a basket which he has just received from Magdalena. Taking advantage of his master's absorption, David examines the ribbons, flowers, cakes, and sausages with which it is stocked, starting guiltily at his master's every movement, and finally seeking to disarm the anger he must feel at the evening's brawl by offering him the gifts he has just received.

Hans Sachs, however, good-naturedly refuses to receive them, and after making his apprentice sing the song for the day he dismisses him to don his festive attire, for he has decided to take him with him to the festival. Left alone, Sachs soliloquises on the follies of mankind, until Walther appears. In reply to his host's polite inquiry how he spent the night, Walther declares he has been visited by a wonderful dream, which he goes on to relate. At the very first words the cobbler discovers that it is part of a beautiful song, conforming to all the Master Singers' rigid rules, and he hastily jots down the words, bidding the young knight be careful to retain the tune.

As they both leave the room to don their festive apparel, Beckmesser comes limping in. He soon discovers the verses on the bench, and pockets them, intending to substitute them for his own in the coming contest. Sachs, coming in, denies all intention of taking part in the day's programme, and when Beckmesser jealously asks why he has been inditing a love song if he does not intend to sue for Eva's hand, he discovers the larceny. He, however, good-naturedly allows Beckmesser to retain the copy of verses, and even promises him that he will never claim the authorship of the song, a promise which Beckmesser intends to make use of so as to pass it off as his own.

Triumphant now and sure of victory, Beckmesser departs as Eva enters in bridal attire. She is of course devoured by curiosity to know what has become of her lover, but, as excuse for her presence, she petulantly complains that her shoe pinches. Kneeling in front of her, Sachs investigates the matter, greatly puzzled at first by her confused and contradictory statements and by her senseless replies to his questions. He is turning his back to the inner door, through which Walther has also entered the shop, but, soon becoming aware of the cause of her perturbation, he deftly draws the shoe from her foot, and going to his last pretends to be very busy over it, while he is in reality listening intently to discover whether Eva's presence will inspire Walther with the third and last verse of his song. His expectations are not disappointed, for the knight, approaching the maiden softly, declares his love in a beautiful song.

As the last notes die away, the cobbler joyfully exclaims that Walther has composed a Master Song, calls Eva and David (who has just entered) as witnesses that he composed it, foretells that, if Walther will only yield to his guidance he will yet enable him to win the prize, and, patting Eva in a truly paternal fashion, he bids her be happy, for she will yet be able to marry the man she loves. David, who has been made journeyman so that he can bear witness for Walther, greets the happy Magdalena with the tidings that they no longer need delay, but can marry immediately.

After the four happy young people and Hans Sachs have given vent to their rapture in a beautiful quintette, they adjourn to the meadow outside of the town, where the musical contest is to take place. The peasants and apprentices are merrily dancing on the green, and cease their mirthful gyrations only when the Master Singers appear. Hans Sachs addresses the crowd, reads the conditions of the test, proclaims what the prize shall be, and concludes by inviting Beckmesser to come forth and begin his song. The young people assembled hail this elderly candidate with veiled scorn, and Beckmesser, painfully clambering to the eminence where the candidates are requested to stand, hesitatingly begins his lay. The words, with which he has had no time to become familiar, are entirely unadapted to his tune, so he draws them out, clips them, loses the thread of the verses, and fails in every sense.

In his chagrin at having made himself ridiculous, and in anger because his colleagues declare the words of his song have no sense, he suddenly turns upon Hans Sachs, and, hoping to humiliate him publicly, accuses him of having written the song. Hans Sachs, of course, disowns the authorship, but stoutly declares the song is a masterpiece, and that he is sure every one present will agree with him if they hear it properly rendered to its appropriate tune. As he is a general favourite among his townsmen, he soon prevails upon them to listen to the author and composer and decide whether he or Beckmesser is at fault.

Walther then springs lightly up the turfy throne, and, inspired by love, he sings with all his heart. The beautiful words, married to an equally beautiful strain, win for him the unanimous plaudits of the crowd, who hail him as victor, while the blushing Eva places the laurel crown upon his head. Pogner, openly delighted with the favourable turn of affairs, gives him the badge of the guild, and heartily promises him the hand of his only daughter. As for Hans Sachs, having publicly proved that his judgment was not at fault, and that he had been keen enough to detect genius even when it revealed itself in a new form, he is heartily cheered by all the Nurembergers, who are prouder than ever of the cobbler poet who has brought about a happy marriage:—
'Hail Sachs! Hans Sachs!
Hail Nuremberg's darling Sachs!'

THE NIBELUNG'S RING.—RHEINGOLD.

It was in 1848, after the completion of Tannhäuser, that Wagner looked about for a subject for a new opera. Then 'for the last time the conflicting claims of History and Legend presented themselves.' He had studied the story of Barbarossa, intending to make use of it, but discarded it in favour of the Nibelungen Myths, which he decided to dramatise.[1] His first effort was an alliterative poem entitled 'The Death of Siegfried,' which, however, was soon set aside, a part of it only being incorporated in 'The Twilight [or Dusk] of the Gods.'

Wagner was then dwelling in Dresden, and planning the organisation of a national theatre; but the political troubles of 1849, which resulted in his banishment, soon defeated all these hopes. After a short sojourn in Paris, Wagner took up his abode in Zurich, where he became a naturalised citizen, and where he first turned all his attention to the principal work of his life,—'The Nibelungen Ring.' In connection with this work Wagner himself wrote: 'When I tried to dramatise the most important moment of the mythos of the Nibelungen in Siegfried's Tod, I found it necessary to indicate a vast number of antecedent facts, so as to put the main incidents in the proper light. But I could only *narrate* these subordinate matters, whereas I felt it imperative that they should be embodied in the action. Thus I came to write Siegfried. But here again the same difficulty troubled me. Finally I wrote "Die Walküre" and "Das Rheingold," and thus contrived to incorporate all that was needful to make the action tell its own tale.' The completed poem was privately printed in 1853, and published 'as a literary product' ten years later, when the author was in his fiftieth year.

As for the score, it was begun in 1853, and Wagner says: 'During a sleepless night at an inn at Spezzia, the music of "Das Rheingold" occurred to me; straightway I turned homeward and set to work.' Such was the energy with which he laboured that the complete score of the Rheingold was finished in 1854. Two years later the music to the Walkyrie was all done, and Siegfried begun. But pecuniary difficulties now forced the master to undertake more immediately remunerative work, and, 'tired of heaping one silent score upon another,' he undertook and finished 'Tristan and Ysolde.' He then thought he would never be able to finish his grand work, and wrote: 'I can hardly expect to find leisure to complete the music, and I have dismissed all hope that I may live to see it performed.'

Fortunately for him, however, Ludwig II. of Bavaria had heard 'Lohengrin' when only sixteen, and, a passionate lover of music and art, he had become an enthusiastic admirer of the great composer. One of the very first acts of his reign was, therefore, to despatch his own private secretary to Wagner with the message, 'Come here and finish your work.'

As this message was backed by a small pension which would enable the musician to keep the wolf from the door, he hopefully went to Munich. But, in spite of the sovereign's continued favour, Wagner found so many enemies that the sojourn there became very unpleasant. It was then that the architect Semper made the first plans for a theatre, in which the king intended that 'The Nibelungen Ring' should be played, as he had formally commissioned Wagner to complete the work.

Driven away from his native land once more by the bitterness of his enemies, Wagner, who still enjoyed Ludwig's entire favour, withdrew in 1865 to Triebschen, where the 'Ring' progressed steadily. It was there, in 1869, that he completed the Siegfried score, and began that of 'The Twilight of the Gods,' which was finished only some time later. As the King's plan for building a national theatre for the representation of 'The Nibelungen Ring' had to be abandoned, the scheme was taken up by the municipality of the little town of Bayreuth. Wagner was cordially invited to take up his residence there, and settled in his new home in 1872, when he was already sixty years of age.

Thanks to munificent private subscriptions secured in great part by the Wagner societies in various parts of the world, the long planned theatre was finally begun. It was finished in 1876, and the entire 'Nibelungen Ring' was performed there in the month of August, the very best singers of the day taking all the principal parts, which they rendered to the best of their abilities. The result was a magnificent performance, a musical triumph; but as the venture was not a financial success, the performances were not repeated in the following summer. Several new ventures, however, were made, and another Wagner festival has just taken place, of which the real result is yet unknown, although the attendance was very large, the audience being composed of people from all parts of the world. Thus Wagner completed and rendered the series of operas, which include plays 'for three days and a fore evening,' whence the series is generally called a 'trilogy,' although it is really composed of four whole operas.

Away down in the translucent depths of the Rhine, three beautiful nymphs, Woglinde, Wellgunde, and Flosshilde, daughters of the river-god, dart in and out among the jagged rocks. They have been stationed there to guard the Rhinegold, the priceless treasure of the deep, whence comes all the warm golden light which illumines the utmost recesses of their dark and damp abode.

The nymphs suddenly pause in their merry game, for the wily dwarf Alberich has emerged from one of the sombre chasms. He is a Nibelung, a spirit of night and darkness, and slowly gropes his way to one of the upper ridges, whence he can see the graceful forms of the nymphs, watch their merry evolutions, and overhear them repeatedly admonish each other to keep watch over the gleaming treasure, which their father, the Rhinegod, has intrusted to their keeping, warning them that just such a dark and misshapen creature as the dwarf would try to wrest it from their grasp:—

'Guard the gold!
Father said
That such was the foe.'

But all Alberich's senses are fascinated by the water-nymphs' beauty, and he soon falls madly in love with them, and makes almost superhuman efforts to overtake the mocking fair. Hotly he pursues them from ridge to ridge, yielding to the blandishments of one after another, and is beside himself with rage as they deftly escape from his clasp just as he fancies he has at last caught them. The fair nymphs, who know they have nothing to fear from so infatuated a lover, swim hither and thither, tantalising him by their nearness, and lure him up and down the rocky river-bed.

They have just exhausted his patience, and driven him wild with impotent rage, when the green waters are suddenly illumined by the phosphorescent glow of the Rhinegold, the treasure whose presence they hail with a rapturous outburst of song, and whose secret power they extol:—

'The realm of the world
By him shall be won
Who from the Rhinegold
Hath wrought the ring
Imparting measureless power.'[2]

The dwarf, attracted by the brilliant light, hears their words at first without paying any attention to them; but when they repeat that he who is willing to forego love can fashion a ring from this gold which will make him master of all the world, he starts with surprise. Fascinated at last by the glow of the treasure, and forgetting all thoughts of love in greed, he suddenly grasps the carelessly guarded gold and plunges with it down into the depths, leaving the three nymphs to bewail its loss in utter darkness.

Little by little the gloom lightens, however, and instead of the river bed the scene represents the green valley through which the Rhine is flowing. In the gray dawn one can descry the high hills on either side, and as the light increases Wotan and Fricka, the principal deities of Northern mythology, are seen lying on the flowery slopes.

As they gently awaken from their peaceful slumbers, the morning mists entirely disappear, revealing in the background the fairy-like beauty of a wondrous palace which has just been completed for their abode. This sight startles Fricka, for she knows that the assembled gods have promised that Fasolt and Fafnir, the gigantic builders, should have sun and moon and the fair Freya as fee. To lose the bright luminaries of the world were bad enough, but Fricka's dismay is still greater at the prospect of parting forever with the fair goddess of beauty and youth. In her sorrow she bitterly regrets that the promise has been made and rendered inviolable by being inscribed on her husband's spear, and reproves him for the joy he shows in viewing the completion of his future abode:—

'In delight thou revel'st
When I am alarmed?
Thou 'rt glad of the fortress,
For Freya I fear.

Bethink thee, thou thoughtless god,
Of the guerdon now to be given!
The castle is finished,
And forfeit the pledge.
Forgettest thou what is engaged?'

Thus suddenly brought to his senses, Wotan, king of the Northern gods, protests that he never really intended to part with the beauty, light, and sweetness of life, and seeks to excuse himself by urging that Loge, the god of fire and the arch-deceiver, overpersuaded him by promising to find some way of escape from the fatal bargain:—

'He whom I hearkened to swore
To find a safety for Freya;
On him my hope have I set.'

They are still discussing the matter, and eagerly wondering why Loge does not appear, when Freya comes rushing wildly upon the stage, with fear-blanched face and trembling limbs, breathlessly imploring the father of the gods to save her from the two huge giants in close pursuit. In her terror she also summons her devoted brothers, Donner and Fro. But, in spite of the strength of these potent gods of the sunshine and thunder, the giants boldly advance, boasting aloud of their achievement, and demanding the fulfilment of the stipulated contract.

The gods are almost at their wits' end with anxiety, when Loge, god of fire, appears. They loudly clamour to him to keep his word and release them from the consequences of their rash bargain. In reply to this summons, Loge declares he has wandered everywhere in search of something more precious than youth and love, and that he has utterly failed to find it. No one, he says, is ready to relinquish these blessed gifts,—no one except Alberich, who has bartered love for the gleaming treasure which he has just stolen from the Rhine nymphs. Loge concludes his speech by delivering to Wotan an imploring message from the defrauded maidens, who summon him to avenge their wrongs and help them to recover the stolen gold. The description of the gleaming treasure, of the power of the ring which Alberich has fashioned out of it, and especially of the immense hoard which he has amassed by the unlimited sway which the ring enables him to wield over all the underground folk, has so greatly fascinated the giants, that, after a few moments' consultation, they step forward, offering to relinquish all claim to the previously promised reward, providing the hoard is theirs ere nightfall. This said, they bear the shrieking and reluctant Freya away as a hostage, and vanish in the distance.

As they depart, the light suddenly grows wan and dim. The goddess who has just departed is the dispenser of the golden apples of perennial youth according to Wagner, and, as she vanishes, the gods, deprived of the substance which keeps them ever young, suddenly lose all their vigour and bloom, and grow visibly old and gray, to their openly expressed dismay:—

'Without the apples,
Old and hoar—
Hoarse and helpless—
Worth not a dread to the world,
The dying gods must grow.'

This sudden change, especially in his beloved wife Fricka, determines Wotan to secure the gold at any price, and he bids Loge lead the way to Alberich's realm, following him bravely down through a deep cleft in the rock, whence rises a dense mist, which soon blots the whole scene from view.

In the mean while, the dwarf Alberich has conveyed the gleaming Rhinegold to his underground dwelling, where, mindful of the nymphs' words, he has forced his brother and slave, the smith Mime, to fashion a ring. No sooner has Alberich put on this trinket than he finds himself endowed with unlimited power, which he uses to oppress all his race, and to pile up a mighty hoard, for the greed of gold has now filled all his thoughts. Fearful lest any one should wrest the precious ring from him, he next directs Mime to make a helmet of gold, the magic tarn-helm, which will render the wearer invisible. Mime is at work at his underground forge, and has just finished the helmet which he intends to appropriate to his own use to escape thraldom, when Alberich suddenly appears, snatches it from his trembling hand, and, placing it upon his head, becomes invisible to all. The malicious dwarf misuses this power to torture Mime with his whip, and rushes off to lash the dwarfs in the rear of the cave as Wotan and Loge suddenly appear. Of course their first impulse is to inquire the cause of Mime's writhing and bitter cries, and from him they hear how Alberich has become lord of the Nibelungs by the might of his ring and magic helmet. In corroboration of this statement, the gods soon behold a long train of dwarfs toiling across the cave, bending beneath their burdens of gold and precious stones, and driven incessantly onward by Alberich's whip, which he plies with merciless vigour. He is visible now, for he has hung the magic helmet to his belt; but he no sooner becomes aware of the gods' presence than he strides up to them, and haughtily demands their name and business. Disarmed a little by Wotan's answer, that they have heard of his new might and have come to ascertain whether the accounts were true, Alberich boasts of his power to compel all to bow before his will, and says he can even change his form, thanks to his magic helmet. At Loge's urgent request, the dwarf then gives them an exhibition of his power by changing himself first into a huge loathsome dragon, and next into a repulsive toad. While in this shape he is made captive by the gods, deprived of his tarn-helm, and compelled to surrender his hoard as the price of his liberty. Before departing, Wotan even wrests from his grasp the golden ring, to which he desperately clings, for he knows that as long as it remains in his possession he will have the power to collect more gold. In his rage at being deprived of it, Alberich hurls his curse after the gods, declaring the ring will ever bring death and destruction to the possessor:—

> 'As by curse I found it first,
> A curse rest on the ring!
> Gave its gold
> To me measureless might,
> Now deal its wonder
> Death where it is worn!'

This curse uttered, he disappears, and while mist invades the place the scene changes, and Loge and Wotan stand once more on the grassy slopes, where Fricka, Donner, and Fro hasten to welcome them, and to inquire concerning the success of their enterprise. Almost at the same moment, the giants Fasolt and Fafnir also appear, leading Freya, whom Fricka would fain embrace, but who is withheld from her longing arms. The grim giants vow that no one shall even touch their fair captive until they have received a pile of gold as high as their staffs, which they drive into the ground, and wide enough to screen the goddess entirely. Thus admonished, Loge and Fro pile up the gleaming treasure, which is surmounted by the glittering helmet, whose power the giants do not know. Freya is entirely hidden, and only a chink remains through which the giants can catch a glimpse of her golden hair. They insist upon having this chink closed up ere they will relinquish Freya, so Wotan is forced to give up the magic ring. But he draws it from his finger only when Erda, the shadowy earth goddess, half rises out of the ground to command the sacrifice of the treasure which Alberich stole from the Rhine maidens.

As the stipulated ransom has all been paid, the giants release Freya. She joyfully embraces her kin, and under her caresses they recover all their former youth and bloom. In the mean while the giants produce their bags, but soon begin quarrelling together about the division of the hoard, and appeal to the gods to decide their dispute. The gods are all too busy to pay any heed to this request, all except the malicious Loge, who slyly advises Fafnir to seize the ring and pay no heed to the rest. As the ring is accursed, Fafnir remorselessly slays his brother to obtain it; then, packing up all the treasure in his great bag, he triumphantly departs. To disperse the shadow hovering over Wotan's brow ever since he has been obliged to sacrifice the ring, Thor now beats the rocks with his magic hammer, and conjures a brief storm. The long roll of thunder soon dies away, and when the fitful play of the lightning is ended Thor shows the assembled gods a glittering rainbow bridge of quivering, changing hues, which stretches from the valley where they are standing to the beautiful portals of the wondrous palace Walhalla, the home of the gods!

Fascinated by this sight, Wotan invites the gods to follow him over its lightly swung arch, and as they trip over the rainbow bridge, the lament of the Rhine-maidens mourning their treasure falls in slow, pitiful cadences upon their ears:—

'Rhinegold!
Purest gold!
O would that thy light
Waved in the waters below!
Unfailing faith
Is found in the deep,
While above, in delight,
Faintness and falsehood abide!'

[1] See the author's 'Myths of Northern Lands' and 'Legends of the Rhine.'
[2] All the quotations in the 'Ring' have been taken either from Dippold's or Forman's admirable translations.

THE WALKYRIE.

Wotan—made secretly uneasy by Erda's dark prediction that

>'Nothing that is ends not;
>A day of gloom
>Dawns for the gods;—
>Be ruled and waive from the ring'—

relinquishes the ring which he had wrested from Alberich, as has been seen. His restlessness however daily increases, until at last he penetrates in disguise into the dark underground world and woos the fair earth goddess. So successfully does he plead his cause, that she receives him as her spouse and bears him eight lovely daughters. She also reveals to him the secrets of the future, when Walhalla's strong walls shall fall, and the gods shall perish, because they have resorted to fraud and lent a willing ear to Loge, prince of evil.

Notwithstanding this fatal prediction Wotan remains undismayed. Instead of yielding passively to whatever fate may befall him, he resolves to prepare for a future conflict, and to defend Walhalla against every foe. As the gods are few in number, he soon decides to summon mortals to his abode, and in order to have men trained to every hardship and accustomed to war, he flings his spear over the world, and kindles unending strife between all the nations. His eight daughters, the Walkyries, are next deputed to ride down to earth every day and bear away the bravest among the slain. These warriors are entertained at his table with heavenly mead, and encouraged to keep up their strength and skill by cutting and hewing each other, their wounds healing magically as soon as made.

But, in spite of these preparations, Wotan is not yet satisfied. He still remembers the all-powerful ring which he has given to the giants, and which is still in the keeping of Fafnir. In case this ring again falls into the hands of the revengeful Alberich, he knows the gods cannot hope to escape from his wrath. He himself cannot snatch back a gift once given, so he decides to beget a son, who will unconsciously be his emissary, and who will, moreover, oppose the offspring which Erda has predicted that Alberich will raise merely to help him avenge his wrongs. Disguised as a mortal named Wälse, or Volsung, Wotan takes up his abode upon earth, and marries a mortal woman, who bears him twin children, Siegmund and Sieglinde. These children are still very young when Hunding, a hunter and lover of strife, comes upon their hut in the woods, and burns it to the ground, after slaying the elder woman and carrying off the younger as his captive.

On their return from the forest, Wälse and Siegmund behold with dismay the destruction of their dwelling, and vow constant warfare against their foes. This vow they faithfully keep until Siegmund grows up and his father suddenly and mysteriously disappears, leaving behind him nothing but the wolf-skin garment to which he owes his name.

Leading him to the oak, she then points out the sword, telling him it was driven into the very heart of the tree by a one-eyed stranger. He had come into the hall on her wedding day, and had declared that none but the mortal for whom the gods intended the weapon would ever be able to pull it out. She then goes on to describe how many strong men have tried to withdraw it, and warmly declares it must have been intended for him who had so generously striven to protect a helpless maiden. Her tender solicitude fills the poor outcast's famished heart with such love and joy that he clasps her to his breast, and, the door swinging noiselessly open to admit a flood of silvery moonbeams, they join in the marvellous duet known as the 'Spring Song.'

As they gaze enraptured upon each other, they too perceive the strong resemblance which has so struck Hunding, but still fail to recognize each other as near of kin. To save Sieglinde from her distasteful compulsory marriage, Siegmund now consents to fly, providing she will accompany him, vowing to protect her till death with the sword which he easily draws from the oak, and which he declares he knows his father must have placed there, as he recognizes him in the description which Sieglinde had given of the stranger:—

'Siegmund the Volsung,
Seest thou beside thee!
For bridal gift
He brings thee this sword.
He woos with the blade
The blissfullest wife.
From the house of the foe
He hies with thee.
Forth from here
Follow him far,
Hence to the laughing
House of the Spring,
Where Nothung the sword defends thee,
Where Siegmund infolds thee in love!'

This passionate appeal entirely sweeps away Sieglinde's last scruples; she yields rapturously to his wooing, and they steal away softly, hand in hand, to go and seek their happiness out in the wide world. Hunding, upon awaking on the morrow, discovers the treachery of his guest and the desertion of his wife. Almost beside himself with fury, he prepares to overtake and punish the guilty pair.

As a fight is now imminent between Siegmund, his mortal son, and Hunding, Wotan, who is up on a rocky mountain overlooking the earth, summons Brunhilde the Walkyrie to his side, bidding her saddle her steed and so direct the battle that Siegmund may remain victor and Hunding only fall. Chanting her Walkyrie war-cry, Brunhilde departs, laughingly calling out to

Wotan that he had best be prepared for a call from his wife, who is hastening toward him as fast as her rams can draw her brazen chariot. Brunhilde has scarcely passed out of sight when Fricka comes upon the scene. After upbraiding Wotan for forsaking her to woo the goddess Erda and a mortal maiden, she says that, as father of the gods and ruler of the world, he is bound to uphold religion and morality. She then dwells angrily upon the immorality of the just consummated union between Siegmund and Sieglinde, who are brother and sister, and finally forces her husband, much against his will, to promise he will revoke his decree, give the victory to the injured husband, Hunding, and punish Siegmund, the seducer, by immediate death.

Wotan therefore summons Brunhilde once more, and sadly bids her to shield Hunding in the coming fight. Brunhilde, who realizes that the second command has been dictated by Fricka, implores him to confide his troubles to her. She then hears with dismay an account of the way in which Wotan has been beguiled into wrongdoing by Loge, of his attempts to gather an army large enough to oppose to his foes when the last day should come, and of his long cherished hope that Siegmund would recover the fatal ring which he feared would again fall into the revengeful Alberich's hands. Finally, however, Wotan repeats his order to her to befriend Hunding, and Brunhilde, awed by his despair, slowly departs to fulfil his commands.

The god has just vanished amid the mutterings of thunder, expressive of his wrath if any one dare to disobey his behests, when Siegmund and Sieglinde suddenly appear upon the mountain side. They are fleeing from Hunding, and Sieglinde, who has discovered when too late that Siegmund is her brother, is so torn by remorse, love, and fear that she soon sinks fainting to the ground. Siegmund, alarmed, bends over her, but, having ascertained that she has only fainted, makes no effort to revive her, deeming it better that she should remain unconscious during the encounter which must soon take place, for the horn of the pursuing Hunding is already heard in the distance.

Siegmund has just pressed a tender kiss upon Sieglinde's fair forehead, when Brunhilde, the Walkyrie, suddenly appears before him, and solemnly warns him of his coming defeat and death. He proudly tells her of his matchless sword, but she informs him that his reliance upon it is quite misplaced, for it will be wrenched from his grasp when his need is greatest. Then she tries to comfort him by describing the glory which awaits him in Walhalla, whither she will convey him after death.

Siegmund eagerly questions her, but, learning that Sieglinde can never be admitted within its shining portals, passionately declares he cannot leave her. He next proposes to kill her and himself, so that they may be together in Hela's dark abode, for he will accept no joys which she cannot share:—

'Then greet for me Valhall,
Greet for me Wotan;
Hail unto Wälse,
And all the heroes!

> Greet, too, the graceful
> Warlike mist-maidens:
> For now I follow thee not.'

Brunhilde's heart is so touched by his love for and utter devotion to Sieglinde, and she is so anxious at the same time to fulfil Wotan's real wish, in defiance of his orders, that she finally allows compassion to get the better of her reason, and impulsively promises Siegmund that she will protect him in the coming fray. At the same moment Hunding's horn is heard, and Brunhilde disappears, while the scene darkens with the rapid approach of a thunderstorm. Such is the darkness that Siegmund, who has sprung down the path in his eagerness to meet his foe, misses his way, while Sieglinde slowly rouses from her swoon, muttering of the days of her happy childhood when she dwelt with her family in the great wood. Suddenly, the lightning flashes, and Hunding and Siegmund, meeting upon a ridge, begin fighting, in spite of Sieglinde's frantic cries.

As the struggle begins, Brunhilde, true to her promise, hovers over the combatants, holding her shield over Siegmund and warding off every dangerous blow, while Sieglinde gazes in speechless terror upon the combatants.

But in the very midst of the fray, when Siegmund is about to pierce Hunding's heart with his glittering sword, Wotan suddenly appears, and, extending his sacred spear to parry the blow, he shivers the sword Nothung to pieces. Hunding basely takes advantage of this accident to slay his defenceless foe, while Brunhilde, fearing Wotan's wrath and Hunding's cruelty, catches up the fainting Sieglinde and bears her rapidly away upon her fleet-footed steed.

After gazing for a moment in speechless sorrow at his lifeless favourite, Wotan turns a wrathful glance upon the treacherous Hunding, who, unable to endure the divine accusation of his unflinching gaze, falls lifeless to the ground. Then the god mounts his steed, and rides off on the wings of the storm in pursuit of the disobedient Walkyrie, whom he is obliged to punish severely for his oath's sake.

The next scene represents an elevated plateau, the trysting spot of the eight Walkyries, on Hindarfiall, or Walkürenfels, whither they all come hastening, bearing the bodies of the slain across their fleet steeds. Brunhilde appears last of all, carrying Sieglinde. She breathlessly pours out the story of the day's adventures, and implores her sisters to devise some means of hiding Sieglinde, and to protect her from Wotan's dreaded wrath:—

> 'The raging hunter
> Behind me who rides,
> He nears, he nears from the North!
> Save me, sisters!
> Ward this woman.'

The sound of the tempest has been growing louder and louder while she is speaking, and as she ends her narrative Sieglinde recovers consciousness, but only to upbraid her for having saved her life. She wildly proposes suicide, until Brunhilde bids her live for the sake of Siegmund's son whom she will bring into the world, and tells her to treasure the fragments of the sword Nothung, which she had carried away. Sieglinde, anxious now to live for her child's sake, hides the broken fragments in her bosom, and, in obedience to Brunhilde's advice, speeds into the dense forest where Fafnir has his lair, and where Wotan will never venture lest the curse of the ring should fall upon him.

'Save for thy son
 The broken sword!
 Where his father fell
 On the field I found it.
 Who welds it anew
 And waves it again,
 His name he gains from me now—
 "Siegfried" the hero be hailed.'

The noise of the storm and rushing wind has become greater and greater, the Walkyries have anxiously been noting Wotan's approach. As Sieglinde vanishes in the dim recesses of the primeval forest, the wrathful god comes striding upon the stage in search of Brunhilde, who cowers tremblingly behind her sisters. After a scathing rebuke to the Walkyries, who would fain shelter a culprit from his all-seeing eye, Wotan bids Brunhilde step forth. Solemnly he then pronounces her sentence, declaring she shall serve him as Walkyrie no longer, but shall be banished to earth, where she will have to live as a mere mortal, and, marrying, to know naught beyond the joys and sorrows of other women:—

'Heard you not how
 Her fate I have fixed?
 Far from your side
 Shall the faithless sister be sundered;
 Her horse no more
 In your midst through the breezes shall haste her;
 Her flower of maidenhood
 Will falter and fade;
 A husband will win
 Her womanly heart,
 She meekly will bend
 To the mastering man
 The hearth she'll heed, as she spins,
 And to laughers is left for their sport.'

Brunhilde, hearing this terrible decree, which degrades her from the rank of a goddess to that of a mere mortal, sinks to her knees and utters a great cry of despair. This is echoed by the Walkyries, who, however, depart at Wotan's command, leaving their unhappy sister alone with him.

Passionately now Brunhilde pleads with her father, declaring she had meant to serve him best by disobeying his commands, and imploring him not to banish her forever from his beloved presence. But, although Wotan still loves her dearly, he cannot revoke his decree, and repeats to her that he will leave her on the mountain, bound in the fetters of sleep, a prey to the first man who comes to awaken her and claim her as his bride.

All Brunhilde's tears and passionate pleadings only wring from him a promise that she will be hedged in by a barrier of living flames, so that none but the very bravest among men can ever come near her to claim her as his own.

Wotan, holding his beloved daughter in a close embrace, then gently seals her eyes in slumber with tender kisses, lays her softly down upon the green mound, and draws down the visor of her helmet. Then, after covering her with her shield to protect her from all harm, he begins a powerful incantation, summoning Loge to surround her with an impassable barrier of flames. As this incantation proceeds, small flickering tongues of fire start forth on every side; they soon rise higher and higher, roaring and crackling until, as Wotan disappears, they form a fiery barrier all around the sleeping Walkyrie:—

'Loge, hear!
Hitherward listen!
As I found thee at first—
In arrowy flame
As thereafter thou fleddest—
In fluttering fire;
As I dealt with thee once,
I wield thee to-day!
Arise, billowing blaze,
And fold in thy fire the rock!
Loge! Loge! Aloft!
Who fears the spike
Of my spear to face,
He will pierce not the planted fire.'

SIEGFRIED.

Sieglinde, having dragged herself into the depths of the great untrodden forest, dwelt there in utter solitude until the time came for her son Siegfried to come into the world. Sick and alone, the poor woman went about in search of aid, and finally came to Mime's cavern, where, after giving birth to her child and intrusting him to the care of the dwarf, she gently breathed her last.

Here, in the grand old forest, young Siegfried grew up to manhood, knowing nothing of his parentage except the lie which Mime, the wily dwarf, chose to tell him, that he was his own son. Strong, fearless, and unruly, the youth soon felt the utmost contempt for the cringing dwarf, and, instead of bending over the anvil and swinging the heavy hammer, he preferred to range the forest, hunting the wild beasts, climbing the tallest trees, and scaling the steepest rocks.

As the opera opens, the curtain rises upon a sooty cave, where the dwarf Mime is alone at work, hammering a sword upon his anvil and complaining bitterly of the strength and violence of young Siegfried, who shatters every weapon he makes. In spite of repeated disappointments, however, Mime the Nibelung works on. His sole aim is to weld a sword which in the bold youth's hands will avail to slay his enemy, the giant Fafnir, the owner of the ring and magic helm, and the possessor of all the mighty hoard.

While busy in his forge, Mime tells how the giant fled with his treasure far away from the haunts of men, concealed his gold in the Neidhole, a grewsome den. There, thanks to the magic helmet, he has assumed the loathsome shape of a great dragon, whose fiery breath and lashing tail none dares to encounter.

As Mime finishes the sword he has been fashioning, Siegfried, singing his merry hunting song, dashes into the cave, holding a bear in leash. After some rough play, which nearly drives the unhappy Mime mad with terror, Siegfried sets the beast free, grasps the sword, and with one single blow shatters it to pieces on the anvil, to Mime's great chagrin. Another weapon has failed to satisfy his needs, and the youth, after harshly upbraiding the unhappy smith, throws himself sullenly down in front of the fire. Mime then cringingly approaches him with servile offers of food and drink, continually vaunting his love and devotion. These protests of simulated affection greatly disgust Siegfried, who is well aware of the fact that they are nothing but the merest pretence.

In his anger against this constant deceit, he finally resorts to violence to wring the truth from Mime, who, with many interruptions and many attempts to resume his old whining tone, finally reveals to him the secret of his birth and the name of his mother. He also tells him all he gleaned about his father, who fell in battle, and, in proof of the veracity of his words, produces the fragments of Siegmund's sword, which the dying Sieglinde had left for her son:—

'Lo! what thy mother had left me!
For my pains and worry together

She gave me this poor reward.
See! a broken sword,
Brandished, she said, by thy father,
When foiled in the last of his fights.'

Siegfried, who has listened to all this tale with breathless attention, interrupting the dwarf only to silence his recurring attempts at self-praise, now declares he will fare forth into the wild world as soon as Mime has welded together the precious fragments of the sword. In the mean while, finding the dwarf's hated presence too unbearable, he rushes out and vanishes in the green forest depths. Left alone once more, Mime wistfully gazes after him, thinking how he may detain the youth until the dragon has been slain. At last he slowly begins to hammer the fragments of the sword, which will not yield to his skill and resume their former shape.

While the dwarf Mime is abandoning himself to moody despair, Wotan has been walking through the forest. He is disguised as a Wanderer, according to his wont, and suddenly enters Mime's cave. The dwarf starts up in alarm at the sight of a stranger, but after asking him who he may be, and learning that he prides himself upon his wisdom, he bids him begone. Wotan, however, who has come hither to ascertain whether there is any prospect of discovering anything new, now proposes a contest of wit, in which the loser's head shall be at the winner's disposal. Mime reluctantly assents, and begins by asking a question concerning the dwarfs and their treasures. This Wotan answers by describing the Nibelungs' gold, and the power wielded by Alberich as long as he was owner of the magic ring.

Mime's second inquiry is relative to the inhabitants of earth, and Wotan describes the great stature of the giants, who, however, were no match for the dwarfs, until they obtained possession not only of the ring, but also of the great hoard over which Fafnir now broods in the guise of a dragon.

Then Mime questions him concerning the gods, but only to be told that Wotan, the most powerful of them all, holds an invincible spear upon whose shaft are engraved powerful runes. In speaking thus the disguised god strikes the ground with his spear, and a long roll of thunder falls upon the terrified Mime's ear.

The three questions have been asked and successfully answered, and it is now Mime's turn to submit to an interrogatory, from which he evidently shrinks, but to which he must yield. Wotan now proceeds to ask him which race, beloved by Wotan, is yet visited by his wrath, which sword is the most invincible of weapons, and who will weld its broken pieces together. Mime triumphantly answers the first two questions by naming the Volsung race and Siegmund's blade, Nothung; but as he has failed to weld the sword anew, and has no idea who will be able to achieve the feat, he is forced to acknowledge himself beaten by the third.

Scorning to take any advantage of so puny a rival, Wotan refuses to take the forfeited head, and departs, after telling the Nibelung that the sword can only be restored to its pristine glory by the hand of a man who knows no fear, and that the same man will claim it as his lawful prize and dispose of Mime's head:—

'Hark thou forfeited dwarf;
None but he
Who never feared,
Nothung forges anew.
Henceforth beware!
Thy wily head
Is forfeit to him
Whose heart is free from fear.'

When Siegfried returns and finds the fire low, the dwarf idle, and the sword unfinished, he angrily demands an explanation. Mime then reveals to him that none but a fearless man can ever accomplish the task. As Siegfried does not even know the meaning of the word, Mime graphically describes all the various phases of terror to enlighten him.

Siegfried listens to his explanations, but when they have come to an end and he has ascertained that such a feeling has never been harboured in his breast, he springs up and seizes the pieces of the broken sword. He files them to dust, melts the metal on the fire, which he blows into an intense glow, and after moulding tempers the sword. While hammering lustily Siegfried gaily sings the Song of the Sword. The blade, when finished, flashes in his hand like a streak of lightning, and possesses so keen an edge that he cleaves the huge anvil in two with a single stroke.

While Siegfried is thus busily employed, Mime, dreading the man who knows no fear, and to whom he has been told his head was forfeit, concocts a poisonous draught. This he intends to administer to the young hero as soon as the frightful dragon is slain, for he has artfully incited the youth to go forth and attack the monster, in hope of learning the peculiar sensation of fear, which he has never yet known.

In another cave, in the depths of the selfsame dense forest, is Alberich the dwarf, Mime's brother and former master. He mounts guard night and day over the Neidhole, where Fafnir, the giant dragon, gloats over his gold. It is night and the darkness is so great that the entrance to the Neidhole only dimly appears. The storm wind rises and sweeps through the woods, rustling all the forest leaves. It subsides however almost as soon as it has risen, and Wotan, still disguised as a Wanderer, appears in the moonlight, to the great alarm of the wily dwarf. A moment's examination suffices to enable him to recognise his quondam foe, whom he maliciously taunts with the loss of the ring, for well he knows the god cannot take back what he has once given away.

Wotan, however, seems in no wise inclined to resent this taunting speech, but warns Alberich of the approach of Mime, accompanied by a youth who knows no fear, and whose keen blade will slay the monster. He adds that the youth will appropriate the hoard, ere he rouses Fafnir to foretell the enemy's coming. Then he disappears with the usual accompaniment of rushing winds and rumbling thunder.

The warning which Alberich would fain disbelieve is verified, as soon as the morning breaks, by the appearance of Siegfried and Mime. The latter is acting as guide, and eagerly points out the mighty dragon's lair. But even then the youth still refuses to tremble, and when Mime describes Fafnir's fiery breath, coiling tail, and impenetrable hide, he good-naturedly declares he will save his most telling blow until the monster's side is exposed, and he can plunge Nothung deep into his gigantic breast.

Thus forewarned against the dragon's various modes of attack, Siegfried advances boldly, while Mime prudently retires to a place of safety. He is closely watched by Alberich, who crouches unseen in his cave. Siegfried seats himself on the bank to wait for the dragon's awakening, and beguiles the time by trying to imitate the songs of the birds, which he would fain understand quite clearly. As all his efforts result in failure, Siegfried soon casts aside the reed with which he had tried to reproduce their liquid notes, and, winding his horn, boldly summons Fafnir to come forth and encounter him in single fight.

This challenge immediately brings forth the frightful dragon. To Siegfried's surprise he can still talk like a man. After a few of the usual amenities, the fight begins. Mindful of his boast, Siegfried skilfully parries every blow, evades the fiery breath, lashing tail, and dangerous claws, and, biding his time, thrusts his sword up to the very hilt in the giant's heart.

With his dying breath, the monster tells the youth of the curse which accompanies his hoard, and, rolling over, dies in terrible convulsions. The young hero, seeing the monster is dead, withdraws his sword from the wound; but as he does so a drop of the fiery blood falls upon his naked hand. The intolerable smarting sensation it produces causes him to put it to his lips to allay the pain. No sooner has he done so than he suddenly becomes aware that a miracle has happened, for he can understand the songs of all the forest birds.

Listening wonderingly, Siegfried soon hears a bird overhead warning him to possess himself of the tarn-helmet and magic ring, and proclaiming that the treasure of the Nibelungs is now his own. He immediately thanks the bird for its advice, and vanishes into the gaping Neidhole in search of the promised treasures:—

'Hi! Siegfried shall have now
The Nibelungs' hoard,
For here in the hole
It awaits his hand!
Let him not turn from the tarn-helm,
It leads to tasks of delight;
But finds he a ring for his finger,
The world he will rule with his will.'

Alberich and Mime, who have been trembling with fear as long as the conflict raged, now timidly venture out of their respective hiding places. Then only they become aware of each other's intention to hasten into the cave and appropriate the treasure, and begin a violent quarrel. It is brought to a speedy close, however, by the reappearance of Siegfried wearing the glittering helmet, armour, and magic ring.

The mere appearance of this martial young figure causes both dwarfs to slink back to their hiding places, while the birds resume their song. They warn Siegfried to distrust Mime, who is even then approaching with the poisonous draught. This the dwarf urges upon him with such persistency that Siegfried, disgusted with his fawning hypocrisy, finally draws his sword and kills him with one blow:—

'Taste of my sword,
Sickening talker!
Meed for hate
Nothung makes;
Work for which he was mended.'

Then, while Alberich is laughing in malicious glee over the downfall of his rival, Siegfried flings his body into the Neidhole, and rolls the dragon's carcass in front of the opening to protect the gold. He next pauses again to listen to the bird in the lime tree, which sings of a lovely maiden surrounded by flames, who can be won as bride only by the man who knows no fear:—

'Ha! Siegfried has slain
The slanderous dwarf.
O, would that the fairest
Wife he might find!
On lofty heights she sleeps,
A fire embraces her hall;
If he strides through the blaze,
And wakens the bride,
Brunhilde he wins to wife.'

This new quest sounds so alluring to Siegfried, that he immediately sets out upon it, following the road which the Wanderer has previously taken. The latter has gone on to the very foot of the mountain, upon which the flickering flames which surrounded Brunhilde are burning brightly. There he pauses to conjure the goddess Erda to appear and reveal future events. Slowly and reluctantly the Earth goddess arises from her prolonged sleep. Her face is pallid as the newly fallen snow, her head crowned with glittering icicles, and her form enveloped in a great white winding-sheet. In answer to the god's inquiries about the future, she bids him question the Norns and Brunhilde. After a few obscure prophecies he allows her to sink down into her grave once more, for he now knows that one of the Volsung race has won the magic ring, and is even now on his way up the mountain to awaken Brunhilde.

In corroboration of these words, Siegfried appears a few moments after the prophetess or Wala has again sunk into rest. Challenged by Wotan the Wanderer, he declares he is on the way to rouse the sleeping maiden. In answer to a few questions, he rapidly adds that he has slain Mime and the dragon, has tasted its blood, and brandishes aloft the glittering sword which has done him good service and which he has welded himself.

Wotan, wishing to test his courage, and at the same time to fulfil his promise to Brunhilde that none should attempt to pass the flames except the one who feared not even his magic spear, now declares that he has slain his father, Siegmund. Siegfried, the avenger, boldly draws his gleaming sword, which, instead of shattering as once before against the divine spear, cuts it to pieces. In the same instant the Wanderer disappears, amid thunder and lightning. Siegfried, looking about him to find Brunhilde, becomes aware of the flickering flames of a great fire, which rise higher and higher as he rushes joyfully into their very midst, blowing his horn and singing his merry hunting lay.

The flames, which now invade the whole stage, soon flicker and die out, and, as the scene becomes visible once more, Brunhilde is seen fast asleep upon a grassy mound. Siegfried comes, and, after commenting upon the drowsing steed, draws nearer still. Then he perceives the sleeping figure in armour, and bends solicitously over it. Gently he removes the shield and helmet, cuts open the armour, and starts back in surprise when he sees a flood of bright golden hair fall rippling all around the fair form of a sleeping woman:—

'No man it is!
Hallowed rapture
Thrills through my heart;
Fiery anguish
Enfolds my eyes.
My senses wander
And waver.
Whom shall I summon
Hither to help me?
Mother! Mother!
Be mindful of me.'

His head suddenly sinks down upon her bosom, but, as her immobility continues, he experiences for the first time a faint sensation of fear. This is born of his love for her, and, in a frantic endeavour to recall her to life, he bends down and kisses her passionately. At the magic touch of his lips, Brunhilde opens her eyes, and, overjoyed at the sight of the rising sun, greets it with a burst of rapturous song ere she turns to thank her deliverer. The first glimpse of the hero in his glittering mail is enough to fill her heart with love, and recognizing in him Siegfried, the hero whose coming she herself has foretold, she welcomes him with joy. Siegfried then relates how he found her, how he delivered her from the fetters of sleep, and, impetuously declaring his passion, claims her love in return.

The scene between the young lovers, the personifications of the Sun and of Spring, is one of indescribable passion and beauty, and when they have joined in a duet of unalterable love, Brunhilde no longer regrets past glories, but declares the world well lost for the love she has won.

> 'Away Walhall's
> Lightening world!
> In dust with thy seeming,
> Towers lie down!
> Farewell greatness
> And gift of the gods!
> End in bliss
> Thou unwithering breed!
> You, Norns, unravel
> The rope of runes!
> Darken upwards
> Dusk of the gods!
> Night of annulment,
> Near in thy cloud!—
> I stand in sight
> Of Siegfried's star;
> For me he was
> And for me he will be,
> Ever and always,
> One and all
> Lighting love
> And laughing death.'

These sentiments are more than echoed by the enamoured Siegfried, who is beside himself with rapture at the mere thought of possessing the glorious creature, who has forgotten all her divine state to become naught but a loving and lovable woman.

DUSK OF THE GODS.

The Norns, or Northern goddesses of fate, are seen in the dim light before dawn, busily weaving the web of destiny on the rocky hillside where the Walkyries formerly held their tryst. As they twist their rope, which is stretched from north to south, they sing of the age of gold. Then they sat beneath the great world-ash, near the limpid well, where Wotan had left an eye in pledge to win a daily draught of wisdom.

They also sing how the god tore from the mighty ash a limb which he fashioned into an invincible spear. This caused the death of the tree, which withered and died in spite of all their care. The third Norn then continues the tale her sisters have begun, and tells how Wotan came home with a shivered spear one day, and bade the gods cut down the tree. Its limbs were piled like fuel all around Walhalla, the castle which the giants had built, and since then Wotan has sat there in moody silence, awaiting the predicted end, which can no longer be far distant.

While they are singing, the barrier of flame in the background burns brightly, and its light grows pale only as dawn breaks slowly over the scene. The rope which the Norns are weaving then suddenly parts beneath their fingers; so they bind the fragments about them and sink slowly into the ground, to join their mother Erda, wailing a prophecy concerning the end of the old heathen world:—

'Away now is our knowledge!
The world meets
From wisdom no more;
Below to Mother, below!'

As they vanish, the day slowly breaks, and Siegfried and Brunhilde come out of the cave. The former is in full armour and bears a jewelled shield, the latter leads her horse, Grane, by the bridle. Tenderly Brunhilde bids her lover farewell, telling him that she will not restrain his ardour, for she knows it is a hero's part to journey out into the world and perform the noble tasks which await him. But her strength and martial fury have entirely departed since she has learned to love, and she repeatedly adjures him not to forget her, promising to await his homecoming behind her flickering barrier of flame, and to think constantly of him while he is away. Siegfried reminds her that she need not fear he will forget her as long as she wears the Nibelung ring, the seal of their troth, and gladly accepts from her in exchange the steed Grane. Although it can no longer scurry along the paths of air, this horse is afraid of nothing, and is ready to rush through water and fire at his command.

As Siegfried goes down the hill leading his steed, Brunhilde watches him out of sight, and it is only when the last echoes of his hunting horn die away in the distance that the curtain falls.

The next scene is played at Worms on the Rhine. Gunther and his sister Gutrune are sitting in their ancestral hall, with their half-brother Hagen. He is the son of Alberich, and has been begotten with the sole hope that he will once help his father to recover the Nibelung ring. Hagen advises Gunther to remember the duty he owes his race, and to marry as soon as possible, and recommends as suitable mate the fair Brunhilde, who is fenced in by a huge barrier of living flame.

Gunther is not at all averse to matrimony, and is anxious to secure the peerless bride proposed, yet he knows he can never pass through the flames, and asks how Brunhilde is to be won. Hagen, who as a Nibelung knows the future, foretells that Siegfried, the dauntless hero, will soon be there, and adds that, if they can only efface from his memory all recollection of past love by means of a magic potion, they can soon induce him to promise his aid in exchange for the hand of Gutrune.

As he speaks, the sound of a horn is heard, and Hagen, looking out, sees Siegfried crossing the river in a boat, and goes down to the landing with Gunther to bid the hero welcome. Hagen leads the horse away, but soon returns, while Gunther ushers Siegfried into the hall of the Gibichungs, and enters into conversation with him. As Siegfried's curiosity has been roused by the strangers calling him by name, he soon inquires how they knew him, and Hagen declares that the mere sight of the tarn-cap had been enough. He then reveals to Siegfried its magical properties, and asks him what he has done with the hoard, and especially with the ring, which he vainly seeks on his hand. Siegfried carelessly replies that the gold is still in the Neidhole, guarded by the body of the dragon, while the ring now adorns a woman's fair hand. As he finishes this statement, Gutrune timidly draws near, and offers him a drinking horn, the draught of welcome, in which, however, the magic potion of forgetfulness has been mixed.

Siegfried drains it eagerly, remarking to himself that he drinks to Brunhilde alone. But no sooner has he partaken of it than her memory leaves him, and he finds himself gazing admiringly upon Gutrune. Gunther then proceeds to tell Siegfried the story of Brunhilde, whom he would fain woo to wife. Although the hero dreamily repeats his words, and seems to be struggling hard to recall some past memory, he does not succeed in doing so. Finally he shakes off his abstraction, and ardently proposes to pass through the fire and win Brunhilde for Gunther in exchange for Gutrune's hand:—

'Me frights not her fire;
I'll woo for thee the maid;
For with might and mind
Am I thy man—
A wife in Gutrun' to win.'

The two heroes now decide upon swearing blood brotherhood according to Northern custom,—an inviolable oath,—and, charging Hagen to guard the hall of the Gibichungs, they immediately sally forth on their quest.

Brunhilde, in the mean while, has remained on the Walkürenfels anxiously watching for Siegfried's return, and spending long hours in contemplating the magic ring, her lover husband's last gift. Her solitude is, however, soon invaded by Waltraute, one of her sister Walkyries. She informs her that Wotan has been plunged in melancholy thought ever since he returned home from his wanderings with a shattered spear, and bade the gods pile the wood of the withered world-ash all around Walhalla. This he has decided shall be his funeral pyre, when the predicted doom of the gods overtakes him.

Waltraute adds also that she alone has found the clue to his sorrow, for she has overheard him mutter that, if the ring were given back to the Rhine-daughters, the curse spoken by Alberich would be annulled, and the gods could yet be saved from their doom:—

'The day the River's daughters
 Find from her finger the ring,
 Will the curse's weight
 Be cast from the god and the world.'

Brunhilde pays but indifferent attention to all this account, and it is only when Waltraute informs her that it is in her power to avert the gods' doom by restoring the ring she wears to the mourning Rhine-daughters, that she starts angrily from her abstraction, swearing she will never part with Siegfried's gift, the emblem and seal of their plighted troth.

Waltraute, seeing no prayers will avail to win the ring, then rides sadly away, while the twilight gradually settles down, and the barrier of flames burns on with a redder glow. At the sound of a hunting horn, Brunhilde rushes joyously to the back of the scene, with a rapturous cry of 'Siegfried!' but shrinks suddenly back in fear and dismay when, instead of the bright beloved form, a dark man appears through the flickering flames. It is Siegfried, who, by virtue of the tarn-helmet, has assumed Gunther's form and voice, and boldly claims Brunhilde as his bride, in reward for having made his way through the barrier of fire. Brunhilde indignantly refuses to recognize him as her master. Passionately kissing her ring, she loudly declares that as long as it graces her finger she will have the strength to repulse every attack and keep her troth to the giver. This declaration so incenses Siegfried—who, owing to the magic potion, has entirely forgotten her and her love—that he rushes towards her, and after a violent struggle wrenches the ring from her finger, and places it upon his own.

Cowed by the violence of this rude wooer, and deprived of her ring, Brunhilde no longer resists, but tacitly yields when he claims her as wife, and both soon disappear in the cave. There Siegfried, mindful of his oath to marry her by proxy only, lays his unsheathed sword between him and his friend's bride:—

'Now, Nothung, witness well
That faithfully I wooed;
Lest I wane in truth to my brother,
Bar me away from his bride!'

Hagen, left alone at Worms to guard the hall of the Gibichungs, is favored in his sleep by a visit from his father, Alberich. The dwarf informs him that ever since the gods touched the fatal ring their power has waned, and that he must do all in his power to recover it from Siegfried, who again holds it, and who little suspects its magic power. As Alberich disappears, carrying with him Hagen's promise to do all he can, the latter awakens just in time to welcome the returning Siegfried. The young hero joyfully announces the success of their expedition, and rapturously claims Gutrune as his bride. After hearing her lover's account of his night's adventures, the maiden leads him into the hall in search of rest and refreshment, while Hagen, summoning the people with repeated blasts of his horn, admonishes them to deck the altars of Wotan, Freya, and Donner, and to prepare to receive their master and mistress with every demonstration of joy. The festive preparations are barely completed, when Gunther and Brunhilde arrive. The bride is pale and reluctant, and advances with downcast eyes, which she raises only when she stands opposite Gutrune and Siegfried, and hears the latter's name. Dropping Gunther's hand, she rushes forward impetuously to throw herself in Siegfried's arms, but, arrested by his cold unrecognising glance, she tremblingly inquires how he came there, and why he stands by Gutrune's side? Calmly then Siegfried announces his coming marriage:—

'Gunther's winsome sister
She that I wed
As Gunther thee.'

Brunhilde indignantly denies her marriage to Gunther, and almost swoons, but Siegfried supports her, and, although Brunhilde softly and passionately asks him if he does not know her, the young hero indifferently hands her over to Gunther, bidding him look after his wife.

At a motion of his hand, Brunhilde's attention is attracted to the ring, and she angrily demands how he dare wear the token which Gunther wrested from her hand.

Bewildered by this question, Siegfried denies ever having received the ring from Gunther, and declares he won it from the dragon in the Neidhole; but Hagen, anxious to stir up strife, interferes, and elicits from Brunhilde an assurance that the hero can have won the ring only by guile.

A misunderstanding now ensues, for while Brunhilde in speaking refers to their first meeting, and swears that Siegfried had wooed and treated her as his wife, he, recollecting only the second encounter, during which he acted only as Gunther's proxy, denies her assertions.

Both solemnly swear to the truth of their statement upon Hagen's spear, calling the vengeance of Heaven down upon them in case of perjury. Then the interrupted wedding festivities are resumed, for Gunther knows only too well by what fraud his bride was obtained, and thinks the transformation has not been complete enough to blind the wise Brunhilde.

As Siegfried gently leads Gutrune away into the hall, whither all but Hagen, Gunther, and Brunhilde follow him, the latter gives way to her extravagant grief. Hagen approaches her, offering to avenge all her wrongs, and even slay Siegfried if nothing else will satisfy her, and wipe away the foul stain upon her honour. But Brunhilde tells him it is quite useless to challenge the hero, for she herself had made him invulnerable to every blow by blessing every part of his body except his back. This she deemed useless to protect, as Siegfried, the bravest of men, never fled from any foe:—

'HAGEN.
So wounds him nowhere a weapon?
BRUNHILDE.

In battle none:—but still
Bare to the stroke is his back
Never—I felt—
In flight he would find
A foe to be harmful behind him,
So spared I his back from the blessing.'

Her resentment against Siegfried has reached such a pitch, however, that she finally hails with fierce joy Hagen's proposal to slay him in the forest on the morrow. Even Gunther acquiesces in this crime, which will leave his sister a widow, and they soon agree that it shall be explained to Gutrune as a hunting casualty.

At noon on the next day Siegfried arrives alone on the banks of the Rhine, in search of a quarry which has escaped him. The Rhine daughters, who concealed it purposely in hopes of recovering their ring, rise up out of the water, and swimming gracefully around promise to help him recover his game if he will only give them his ring. Siegfried, who attaches no value whatever to the trinket, but wishes to tease them, refuses it at first; but when they change their bantering into a prophetic tone and try to frighten him by telling him the ring will prove his bane unless he intrust it to their care, he proudly answers that he has never yet learned to fear, and declares he will keep it, and see whether their prediction will be fulfilled:—

'My sword once splintered a spear;—
The endless coil
Of counsel of old,
Wove they with wasting
Curses its web;

Norns shall not cover from Nothung!
One warned me beware
Of the curse a Worm;
But he failed to make me to fear,—
The World's riches
I won with a ring,
That for love's delight
Swiftly I'd leave;
I'll yield it for sweetness to you;
But for safety of limbs and of life,—
Were it not worth
Of a finger's weight,—
No ring from me you will reach!'

The Rhine maidens then bid him farewell, and swim away repeating their ominous prophecy. After they have gone, the hunting party appear, heralded by the merry music of their horns. All sit down to partake of the refreshments that have been brought, and as Siegfried has provided no game, he tries to do his share by entertaining them with tales of his early youth.

After telling them of his childhood spent in Mime's forge, of the welding of Nothung and the slaying of Fafnir, he describes how a mere taste of the dragon's blood enabled him to understand the songs of the birds. Encouraged by Hagen, he next relates the capture of the tarn-helm and ring, and then, draining his horn in which Hagen has secretly poured an antidote to the draught of forgetfulness administered by Gutrune, he describes his departure in quest of the sleeping Walkyrie and his first meeting with Brunhilde. At the mere mention of her name, all the past returns to his mind. He suddenly remembers all her beauty and love, and starts wildly to his feet, but only to be pierced by the spear of the treacherous Hagen, who had stolen behind him to drive it into his heart.

The dying hero makes one last vain effort to avenge himself, then sinks feebly to the earth, while Hagen slips away, declaring that the perjurer had fully deserved to be slain by the weapon upon which he had sworn his false oath. Gunther, sorry now that it is too late, bends sadly over the prostrate hero, who, released from the fatal effects of Gutrune's draught, speaks once more of his beloved Brunhilde, and fancies he is once more clasped in her arms as of old.

Then, when he has breathed his last, the hunters place his body upon a shield and bear it away in the rapidly falling dusk, to the slow, mournful accompaniment of a funeral march, whose muffled notes fall like a knell on the listener's ear.

Gutrune, who has found the day very long indeed without her beloved Siegfried, comes out of her room at nightfall, and listens intently for the sound of the hunting horn which will proclaim his welcome return. She is not the only watcher, however, for Brunhilde has stolen down to the river, and her apartment is quite empty.

Suddenly Hagen comes in, and Gutrune, terrified at his unexpected appearance, anxiously inquires why she has not heard her husband's horn. Without any preparation, roughly, brutally, Hagen informs her the hero is dead, just as the bearers enter and deposit his lifeless body at her feet.

Gutrune faints, but when she recovers consciousness she indignantly refuses to credit Hagen's story, that her husband was slain by a boar. She wildly accuses Gunther, who frees himself from suspicion by denouncing Hagen. Without showing the least sign of remorse, the dark son of Alberich then acknowledges the deed, and, seeing that Gunther is about to appropriate the fatal ring, draws his sword and slays him also. Wildly now Hagen snatches at the ring, that long coveted treasure; but he starts back in dismay without having secured it, for the dead hand is threateningly raised, to the horror of all the spectators.

Next Brunhilde comes upon the scene, singing a song of vengeance; and when Gutrune wildly accuses her of being the cause of her husband's murder, she declares that she alone was Siegfried's lawful wife, and that he would always have been true to her had not Gutrune won him by the ruse of a magic draught. Sadly Gutrune acknowledges the truth of this statement, and, feeling that she has no right to mourn over the husband of another woman, she creeps over to Gunther's corpse and bends motionless over him.

Brunhilde's anger is all forgotten now that the hero is dead, and, after caressing him tenderly for a while, she directs the bystanders to erect a huge funeral pyre. While they are thus occupied she sings the hero's dirge, and draws the ring unhindered from his dead hand. Then she announces her decision to perish in the flames beside him, and declares the Rhine maidens can come and reclaim their stolen treasure from their mingled ashes:—

'Thou guilty ring!
Running gold!
My hand gathers,
And gives thee again.
You wisely seeing
Water sisters,
The Rhine's unresting daughters,
I deem your word was of weight!
All that you ask
Now is your own;
Here from my ashes'
Heap you may have it!—
The flame as it clasps me round
Free from the curse of the ring!—
Back to its gold
Unbind it again,
And far in the flood
Withhold its fire,
The Rhine's unslumbering sun,

That for harm from him was reft.'

The curse of the ring is at an end. The ravens of Wotan, perching aloft, fly heavily off to announce the tidings in Walhalla, while Brunhilde, after seeing Siegfried's body carefully deposited on the pyre with all his weapons, kindles the fire with her own hand. Then, springing upon Grane, she rides into the very midst of the flames, which soon rise so high that they swallow her up and entirely hide her from the spectators' sight.

After a short time the flames die down, the bright light fades, the stage darkens, and the river rises and overflows its banks, until its waves come dashing over the funeral pyre. They bear upon their swelling crests the Rhine maidens who have come to recover their ring, Hagen, standing gloomily in the background, becomes suddenly aware of their intention, wildly flings his weapons aside, and rushes forward, crying, 'Unhand the ring!' But he is caught in the twining arms of two of the Rhine maidens, who draw him down under the water, and drown him, while the third, having secured the Nibelung ring, returns in triumph on the ebbing waves to her native depths, chanting the Rhinegold strain. As she disappears, a reddish glow like the Aurora Borealis appears in the sky. It grows brighter and brighter, until one can discern the shining abode of Walhalla, enveloped in lurid flames from the burning world-ash, and in the centre the assembled gods calmly seated upon their thrones, to submit to their long predicted doom, the 'Götterdämmerung.'[3]

[3] See Prof. G.T. Dippold's 'Ring of the Nibelung.'

PARSIFAL.

It was while he was searching for the material for Tannhäuser, that Wagner came across Wolfram von Eschenbach's poems of 'Parsifal' and 'Titurel,'[4] and, as he reports, 'an entirely new world of poetical matter suddenly opened before me.' Wagner made no use of this idea, however, until 1857, some fifteen years later, when he drew up the first sketch of his Parsifal, during his residence at Zurich; twenty years later he finished the poem at Bayreuth. He then immediately began the music, although he was sixty-five years of age. That same year, while he was making a concert tour in London, he read the poem to a select audience of friends, by whose advice it was published.

Although the music for this opera, which is designated as 'a solemn work destined to hallow the stage,' was finished in 1879, the instrumentation was completed only in 1882, at Palermo, a few months before its first production at Bayreuth.

This opera, which Wagner himself called a religious drama, is intended as the 'Song of Songs of Divine Love, as Tristan and Ysolde is the Song of Songs of Terrestrial Love.' The performance was repeated sixteen times at Bayreuth, where many people had come from all parts of the world to hear and see it, and has since been revived a number of times. It is the most difficult and least easily understood of the master's intricate works, and bears the imprint not only of his philosophical studies, but also of the spirit of Oriental mysticism, in which he delighted, and which he at one time intended to make use of for the stage.

The opera opens in the forest, where Gurnemanz, an old servant of Amfortas, guardian of the Holy Grail, is lying asleep with two squires. Suddenly, reveille sounds from the top of Mount Salvat, the sacred hill upon which the temple stands. Gurnemanz, springing to his feet, rouses the squires, and bids them prepare the bath for their ailing master, who will soon appear as is his daily custom.

This Amfortas, whose coming they momentarily expect, is the son of Titurel, the founder of the temple erected on Mount Salvat for the reception of the Holy Grail, a vessel in which Joseph of Arimathea caught a few drops of blood from the dying Redeemer's side, after it had served as chalice during the Last Supper. Titurel, feeling too old to continue his office as guardian of the Grail, appointed Amfortas as his successor, giving him the sacred lance which pierced the Saviour's side, and told him that none could resist him as long as he wielded it and kept himself perfectly pure.

During many years Amfortas led a stainless life, defending the Holy Grail from every foe, performing all his sacred offices with exemplary piety, and teaching the Knights of the Grail to fight for the right, and rescue the feeble and oppressed. He also sent out messengers to all parts of the world to right the wrong, whenever called upon to do so, by the words which suddenly appeared and glowed like fire around the edge of the mystic vase. All the knights who served the Holy Grail were not only fed with celestial viands by its power alone, but were endowed with resistless might, which assured their victory everywhere as long as they remained unknown. They had moreover the privilege of recovering, as if by magic, from every wound. Of course, many knights were desirous of being admitted into the temple, but none except those whose lives were pure and whose purposes lofty were ever accepted. When Klingsor, the magician, attempted to enter, therefore, he was repulsed. In his anger he established himself upon the other side of the mountain, where, summoning all the arts of magic to his aid, he called up delusions of every kind. Thus he beguiled many of the knights in search of the Holy Grail, caught them in his toils and led them on to sin, until they were unfit for the holy life to which they had once aspired.

Amfortas, hearing of this, and too confident in his own strength, sallied forth one day, armed with the sacred lance, determined to destroy Klingsor, and put an end to his magic. But alas! he had no sooner entered the magician's garden, where roamed a host of lovely maidens trained to lure all men to sin, than he yielded to the blandishments of the fairest among them. Carelessly flinging his sacred lance aside, he gave himself up to the delights of passion. Such was his bewitched condition that he never even noticed the stealthy approach of the magician, who seized the lance and thrust it into his side. This deep wound, which had refused to heal ever since, caused him incessant tortures, which were increased rather than diminished whenever he uncovered the Holy Grail.

Although no remedy could allay this torture, the Holy Grail decreed that it should be stilled by a guileless fool, who, enlightened by pity, would find the only cure. But, as he tarried, many knights travelled all over the world in search of simples, and Kundry, a wild, witch-like woman, also sought in vain to relieve him.

While the squires, in obedience to Gurnemanz's orders, prepare the bath, Kundry comes riding wildly on the scene. In breathless haste she thrusts a curious little flask into Gurnemanz's hand, telling him it is a precious balsam she has brought from a great distance to alleviate Amfortas's suffering. She is so exhausted by her long ride that she flings herself upon the ground, where she remains while a little procession comes down the hill. It is composed of knights bearing the wounded Amfortas, and they set the litter down for a moment, as the king gives vent to heart-rending groans. To soothe him, his attendants remind him that there are many more remedies to try, and Gurnemanz adds that, failing all others, they can always rely upon the promise of the Holy Grail, and await the coming of the guileless fool. When Amfortas learns that Kundry has made another attempt to help him, he thanks her kindly, but his gentle words only seem to increase her distress, for she writhes uneasily on the ground and refuses all thanks.

When the king and his bearers have gone down the hill, and have passed out of sight, the squires begin chaffing poor Kundry. She gazes upon them with the wild eyes of an animal at bay, until Gurnemanz comes to her rescue, and chides the youths. He tells them that although she may once have been, as they declare, under a curse, she has repented of her sins, and serves the Holy Grail with a humility and singleness of purpose which they would do well to imitate rather than deride.

In answer to their questions, he then goes on to describe how Amfortas received the grievous wound which causes him such intolerable pain, and lost the sacred spear, which only enhances Klingsor's power for evil, and which none but a stainless knight can ever recover. Their quiet conversation is brusquely interrupted by the heavy fall of a swan, which lies dead at their feet. This arouses their keenest indignation, for the rules of the order forbid any deed of violence within sight or hearing of the sacred edifice containing the Holy Grail. Gazing around in search of the culprit, they soon behold the youth Parsifal, clad in the rough and motley garments of a fool, and when Gurnemanz angrily reproves him, and questions him concerning his name and origin, he is amazed by the ignorance the lad displays.

By the help of Kundry, however, who, having travelled everywhere, knows everything, Gurnemanz finally ascertains that the youth is a descendant of the royal family, his father, Gamuret, having died when he was born. His mother, Herzeloide (Heart's Affliction), has brought him up in utter solitude and ignorance, to prevent his becoming a knight and leave her perchance to fall in battle:—

'Bereft of father his mother bore him.
For in battle perished Gamuret:
From like untimely hero's death
To save her offspring, strange to arms
She reared him a witless fool in deserts.'

The youth, however, pays no heed to Kundry's explanations, but goes on to tell Gurnemanz that he saw some men riding through the forest in glittering array, and followed them through the world with no other weapon than the bow he had manufactured. But when Kundry again interrupts him, declaring that his sudden disappearance has caused his mother's death, he shows the greatest sensibility, and even faints with grief.

While the squires gently bathe his face and hands to bring him back to life, Kundry, feeling the sudden and overpowering desire for sleep which often mysteriously overpowers her, creeps reluctantly into a neighbouring thicket, where she immediately sinks into a comatose state. In the mean while, the king's procession comes up from the bath, and slowly passes across the stage and up the hill. Gurnemanz, whose heart has been filled with a sudden hope that the youth before him may be the promised guileless fool who alone can cure the king, puts an arm around him, gently raises him, and, supporting his feeble footsteps, leads him up the hill. They walk along dark passages, and finally come into the great hall on the top of Mount Salvat, which is empty now, and where only the sound of the bells in the dome is heard as Gurnemanz says to Parsifal:—

'Now give good heed, and let me see,
If thou 'rt a Fool and pure
What wisdom thou presently canst secure.'

    Parsifal, the unsophisticated youth, stands spellbound at the marvels he beholds, nor does he move when the great doors open, and the Knights of the Grail come marching in, singing of the mystic vessel and of its magic properties. This strain is taken up not only by the youths who follow them, but also by a boy choir in the dome which is intended to represent the angels. When the knights have all taken their places, the doors open again to admit the bearers of the sacred vessel, which is kept in a shrine. They are followed by Amfortas, in his litter, and when he has been carefully laid upon a couch, and the vessel has been placed upon the altar before him, all bow down in silent prayer. Suddenly the silence is broken by the voice of the aged Titurel. He is lying in a niche in the rear of the hall, and calls solemnly upon his son to uncover the Holy Grail, and give him a sight of the glorious vessel, which alone can renew his failing strength. The boys are about to remove the veil when Amfortas suddenly detains them, and begins a passionate protest, relating how his sufferings increase every time he beholds the Grail. He implores his father to resume the sacred office, and wildly asks how long his sufferings must endure. To this appeal the angels' voices respond by repeating the prophecy made by the Holy Grail:—

'By pity 'lightened
The guileless Fool—
Wait for him
My chosen tool.'

    Strengthened by this reminder of ultimate relief, and by the voice of the knights and of Titurel again calling for the uncovering of the Grail, Amfortas takes the crystal cup from its shrine, bends over it in devout prayer, while the angel voices above chant a sort of communion service, and the hall is gradually darkened. Suddenly a beam of blinding light shoots down through the dome and falls upon the cup, which 'glows with an increased purple lustre,' while Amfortas holds it above his head, and gently waves it to and fro, so that its mystic light can be seen by all the knights and squires, who have sunk to their knees.
    Titurel hails the sight with a pious ejaculation, and when Amfortas has replaced the vessel in the shrine the beam of light disappears, daylight again fills the hall, and knights and squires begin to partake of the bread and wine before them, a feast to which Gurnemanz invites the amazed Parsifal by a mute gesture. The youth is too astonished to accept; he remains spellbound, while the invisible choir resume their chant, which is taken up first by the youths' voices, and then by the knights, and ends only as the meal draws to a close, and Amfortas is

borne out, preceded by the Holy Grail and followed by the long train of knights and squires.

Gurnemanz and Parsifal alone remain. The Fool, though guileless, has not been enlightened by pity to inquire the cause of Amfortas's wound. He has thus missed his opportunity to cure him, and Gurnemanz, indignant at his boundless stupidity, opens a side door, and thrusts him out into the forest, uttering a contemptuous dismissal.

> 'Thou art then nothing but a Fool!
> Come away, on thy road be gone
> And put my rede to use:
> Leave all our swans for the future alone
> And seek thyself, gander, a goose.'

The second act represents the inner keep of Klingsor's castle, the magician himself being seated on the battlement. He is gazing intently into the magic mirror, wherein all the world may be seen, and comments with malicious glee upon Parsifal's ejection from the temple of the Holy Grail and his approach to his enchanted ground.

Laying aside his magic mirror, Klingsor then begins one of his uncanny spells, and in the midst of a bluish vapor calls up Kundry from the enchanted sleep into which his art has bound her. He tells her that, although she has succeeded in escaping his power for a short time, and has gone over to the enemy whom she has done all in her power to serve, he now requires her to exercise all her fascinations to beguile Parsifal away from the path of virtue, as she once lured Amfortas, the king and guardian of the Holy Grail.

In vain the half awakened Kundry struggles and tries to resist his power, Klingsor has her again in his toils, and once more compels her, much against her wishes, to execute his will. Just as Parsifal, overcoming all resistance, drives away the guards of the castle and springs up on the ramparts, the magician waves his wand. He and his tower sink from view, and a beautiful garden appears, in which lovely damsels flit excitedly about in very scanty attire. After a few moments spent in motionless admiration of the scene before him, Parsifal springs down into the garden, where he is immediately surrounded by the fair nymphs. They pull him this way and that, tease and cajole him, and use all their wiles to attract his attention and win his admiration. Seeing him very indifferent to their unadorned charms, a few of them hastily retire into a bower, where they don gay flower costumes, in which they soon appear before him, winding in and out in the gay mazes of the dance.

Their youthful companions immediately follow their example, and also try to beguile Parsifal by their flower hues, their kisses and caresses, but he stands stolidly by until Kundry, who is now no longer a terrible and haggard witch, but a fair enchantress reclining upon a bed of roses, calls him to her side.

As in a dream, Parsifal obeys her summons, while the flower nymphs flit away to their respective bowers. Wonderingly he now inquires how Kundry knows his name, and again hears her relate how she was present at his birth, watched over his childhood, and witnessed the death of his mother. At this mention the youth is again overcome with grief. To comfort him, Kundry, the enchantress, tenderly embraces him, and lavishes soft words upon him, but all her caresses have no effect, except to awaken in his heart a sudden miraculous comprehension of all he has seen. Love is suddenly born in his heart, but it is not the evil passion which Kundry had striven to bring to life, but the pure, unselfish feeling which enables one human being to understand and sympathise with another. He now knows that Amfortas yielded to passion's spell, and in punishment suffered the spear wound in his side, and realizes that he alone could have given him relief. Moved to sudden indignation by his compassion, he flings Kundry's caressing arms aside, promising, however, to help her win her own redemption, if she will only tell him how to save Amfortas, and will reveal who wielded the spear which dealt the fatal wound. But Kundry, who is acting now entirely under Klingsor's influence, and not by her own volition, seeing she cannot lure him to sin, and that he is about to escape forever, shrieks frantically for help, cursing him vehemently, and declaring that he will have to wander long ere he can again find a way to the realm of the Holy Grail. Her piercing screams bring the flower damsels and Klingsor upon the scene, and the latter, standing upon the rampart, flings the holy spear at Parsifal, expecting to wound him as grievously as Amfortas. But the youth has committed no sin, he is quite pure; so the spear remains poised above his head, until he stretches out his hand, and, seizing it, makes a sign of the cross, adjuring the magic to cease:—

'This sign I make, and ban thy cursed magic:
 As the wound shall be closed
 Which thou with this once clovest,—
 To wrack and to ruin
 Falls thy unreal display!'

At the holy sign, the enchanter's delusions vanish, maidens and gardens disappear, and Kundry sinks motionless upon the arid soil, while Parsifal springs over the broken wall, calling out that they shall meet again.

The third act is played also upon the slopes of the mountain, upon which the temple stands. Many years have elapsed, however, and Gurnemanz, bent with age, slowly comes out of his hut at the sound of a groan in a neighbouring thicket. The sounds are repeated until the good old man, who has assumed the garb of a hermit, searches in the thicket, and, tearing the brambles aside, finds the witch Kundry in one of her lethargic states. He has seen her so before in days gone by, and, dragging her rigid form out from the thicket, he proceeds to restore her to life. Wildly as of old her eyes roll about, but she has no sooner come to her senses than she clamours for some work to do for the Holy Grail, and proceeds to draw water and perform sundry menial tasks. Gurnemanz, watching her closely, comments upon her altered behaviour, and expresses a conviction that she will ultimately be saved, since she has returned to the Grail after many years on the morning of Good Friday.

He is so occupied in examining her that he does not notice the approach of Parsifal, clad in black armour, with closed helmet and lowered spear, and it is only when Kundry calls his attention to the stranger that he welcomes him, but without recognizing him in the least.

Parsifal, however, has not forgotten the old man whom he has sought so long in vain, and is, so overcome by emotion that he cannot speak. He obeys Gurnemanz's injunctions to remove his arms, as none dare enter the holy precincts of the Holy Grail in martial array, and, planting the spear he recovered from Klingsor into the ground, he bends the knee before it, and returns silent thanks that his quest is ended, and he may at last be vouchsafed to quiet the pain which Amfortas still endures. While he is wrapt in prayer, Gurnemanz, staring at him, suddenly recognizes him as the Guileless Fool who came so long ago, and imparts his knowledge to Kundry, who confirms it. Parsifal, having finished his prayer, and recovered the power of speech, now greets Gurnemanz, and in answer to his question says that he has wandered long, and expresses a fervent hope that he has not come too late to retrieve his former fault:—

'Through error and through suffering lay my pathway;
May I believe that I have freed me from it,
Now that this forest's murmur
Falls upon my senses,
And worthy voice of age doth welcome?
Or yet—is 't new error?
All's altered here meseemeth.'

Gurnemanz is almost overcome with joy when he hears the young man declare that he has brought back the sacred lance undefiled, although he has suffered much to defend it from countless foes who would fain have wrested it from him. As Parsifal now begins eagerly to question him, he mournfully relates that times have changed indeed. Amfortas still lives, and suffers untold tortures from his unhealed wound, but Titurel, the aged king, no longer quickened by the sight of the Holy Grail, (which has never again been unveiled since his unhappy visit,) has slowly passed away, and has closed his eyes in a last sleep. At these sad tidings Parsifal faints with remorse, and Gurnemanz and Kundry restore him with water from the holy spring, with which they also wash away all the soil of travel. As he comes to life again, inquiring whether he will be allowed to see Amfortas, Gurnemanz tells him that the knights are to assemble once more in the temple, as of old, to celebrate Titurel's obsequies, and that Amfortas has solemnly promised to unveil the Holy Grail, although at the cost of suffering to himself. He wishes to comfort the knights, who have lost all their courage and strength, and are no longer called upon to go forth and battle for the right in the name of the Grail.

To enable Parsifal to appear in the temple, Gurnemanz now baptises him with water from the spring, and Kundry, anointing his feet with a costly perfume, wipes them with her hair. Parsifal rewards her for this humble office by baptising her in his turn. Then Gurnemanz anoints Parsifal's head with the same ointment, for it is decreed he shall be king, and after he and Kundry have helped him to don the usual habit of the servants of the Holy Grail they proceed, as in the first act, to the temple, and once more enter the great hall.

As they appear, the doors open, and two processions enter, chanting a mournful refrain. Ten knights bear the bier containing Titurel's corpse, the others carry the wasted form of the wounded king. The chorus ended, the coffin is opened, and at the sight of the dead Titurel all the assistants cry out in distress. No wail is so bitter, however, as that of Amfortas, who mournfully addresses his dead father, imploring him to intercede for him before the heavenly throne, and to obtain for him the long hoped for and long expected release.

Then he bids the knights uncover the Holy Grail; but ere they can do so he bursts out into a paroxysm of grief, exposing his bleeding and throbbing wound, and declaring he has not the courage to endure the sacred beam of light from the Holy Grail. But, unnoticed by all, Parsifal, Gurnemanz, and Kundry have drawn near. Suddenly the youth extends the sacred spear, and, touching Amfortas with its point, declares that its power alone can stanch the blood and heal the wounded side, and pronounces the absolution of his sin:—

'Be whole, unsullied and absolved,
For I now govern in thy place.
Oh blessed be thy sorrows,
For Pity's potent might
And Knowledge's purest power
They taught a timid Fool.'

No sooner has the sacred point touched the wound than it is indeed healed, and while Amfortas sinks tottering with emotion into the arms of Gurnemanz, all the knights gaze enraptured at the spear. Then Parsifal announces that he is commanded by Divine decree to become the guardian of the Grail, which he unveils and reverently receives into his hands.

Once more the hall is darkened, once more the beam of refulgent light illumines the gloom, and, as Parsifal slowly waves the vessel to and fro, a snowy dove, the emblem of the Holy Grail, hovers lightly over his head.

Suddenly the beam of light falls across the face of the dead Titurel, who, coming to life again in its radiance, raises his hand in fervent blessing ere he sinks back once more to peaceful rest. Kundry, too, has seen the Holy Grail before her eyes closed in death, and Amfortas, cured and forgiven, joins the knights and invisible choir in praising God for his great mercy, which endures forever.

[4] See the author's 'Legends of the Middle Ages,' in press.

Lightning Source UK Ltd.
Milton Keynes UK
08 February 2010

149762UK00003B/105/A